INVISIBLE
SCARS
of
WAR

INVISIBLE
SCARS
of
WAR

A Veteran's Struggle with Moral Injury

DICK HATTAN

WOODSTOCK SQUARE PRESS

Invisible Scars of War: *A Veteran's Struggle with Moral Injury*

Woodstock Square Press

ISBN: 978-1-7327410-0-3 (Paperback)
ISBN: 978-1-7327410-1-0 (Ebook)

Printed in the United States of America

Madalyn Stone, Editor

Cover and interior book design by Jerry Dorris, www.authorsupport.com

Contents

Preface   ix

Introduction   xv

CHAPTER 1: *I Am a Patriot*   1

CHAPTER 2: *Mount Greenwood*   5

CHAPTER 3: *College—And then What?*   13

CHAPTER 4: *A Plumber's Apprentice*   15

CHAPTER 5: *Other Options*   19

CHAPTER 6: *Seminary Days*   23

CHAPTER 7: *What Does the Church Say?*   27

CHAPTER 8: *1-A*   33

CHAPTER 9: *Basic Training—Fort Dix, New Jersey*   39

CHAPTER 10: *Mental Preparation*   47

CHAPTER 11: *Conscientious Objector*   51

CHAPTER 12: *A "Just War": Was the War in Vietnam Just?*   55

CHAPTER 13: *Thou Shalt Not Kill*   65

CHAPTER 14: *An AWOL God*   73

CHAPTER 15: *Phu Bai*   81

CHAPTER 16: *The Phu Bai Chapel*   89

CHAPTER 17: *My New Block*   95

CHAPTER 18: *The Bob Hope Show*   103

CHAPTER 19: *Returning Home*   107

CHAPTER 20: *A Wounded Soul*   113

CHAPTER 21: *Soul Repair*   119

CHAPTER 22: *Gooks*   123

CHAPTER 23: *Soul Fragmentation*   127

CHAPTER 24: *Forgiveness*   133

CHAPTER 25: *Questions, Questions*   139

CHAPTER 26: *No, Thanks!*   141

CHAPTER 27: *Healing*   143

CHAPTER 28: *Parker Palmer and Discovering My Calling*   147

CHAPTER 29: *The Order of St. Luke and My Focus on Healing*   151

CHAPTER 30: *Ken Burns at the Union League Club of Chicago: PBS on Viet Nam*   155

CONCLUSION   161

Acknowledgments   167

Bibliography   169

*"What obligation did a citizen owe his country?
What should one do when asked to fight a
war in which one did not believe?"*

~Tim O'Brien,
The Vietnam War: An Intimate History

PREFACE

I didn't plan to write a book about moral injury or about how I felt about serving in the US Army in the Vietnam War. The story seemed to grow around me, over me, and through me like "Creeping Charlie" (the ground cover, not the slang expression for a Vietcong intruder). I started keeping a journal in the midstages of my business career in order to relieve stress and shed light on the hypocrisy and mean-spiritedness of life in the nonprofit hospital boardroom. It was despicable to me that physicians used their influence as board members and members of the medical staff to defame their colleagues and disrupt the medical community to protect their medical practices and discourage competition. It was equally reprehensible that conscientious, community-minded businesspeople sought leadership positions in the hospitals where they served as board members when executive salaries became competitive with the private sector.

These and other stories of unethical behavior drove me to chronicle my thoughts for self-therapy as I witnessed this happening around me. The therapy came from the physical act of writing—watching the ink flow onto the blank page, filling it to the point of overflowing. I've saved these journals and occasionally revisit the issues that confronted me during those times of my life. I marvel about how good situations turned sour and how great career opportunities fell apart; either through influences outside my control or because of my own naiveté or inexperience. What I found helpful in the midst of the exhilaration and deep sorrow was my ability to sort out my feelings and set a new course for myself by expressing these emotions in living color.

I occasionally wrote about my military career, but it wasn't until I was asked to join an advisory committee that oversaw a federal grant that provided funding for mental health services for veterans and their families that I got serious about writing my story. On the advisory committee, I was sitting there voting for programs for veterans and trying to appear intelligent by occasionally asking a few questions. But I wasn't doing anything on a personal level with the veterans who were returning from overseas assignments. I read and heard about them and their issues, but I had no skin in the game.

A colleague whom I met through a community leadership program encouraged me to join her in proposing and raising funds for the creation of a writing workshop where veterans could tell their stories. The simplicity of the venture was the key to its success. There were no salaries to be considered, no employees, and no initial budget, except for a few books we purchased as examples of the writing we would do. We just got together twice a month and wrote about our experiences and shared the stories in the safety of our group. The program, Voices of Veterans, took off, and over the past seven years has welcomed over twenty-five veterans from every war from World War II to Operation Iraqi Freedom.

The irony of it was that while I was helping people write their stories, I also began to write my own. As we talked about and wrote about our military experiences, I was finding a safe haven for the thoughts and fears I had tucked away deep within my subconscious. I discovered acceptance among a group of veterans I had not known before, but who treated me like a brother and who have become an amazing byproduct of friendship and support through the entire experience of writing together.

I always knew that there was something deep inside that wanted to see the light of day, something that needed to be expressed and forgiven. It was this need for forgiveness that pushed me to open Pandora's box and examine the conflict that I was feeling in my soul. I didn't realize that my soul was troubled. It was during my graduate studies at Chicago Theological Seminary (CTS) that I came to realize that a transformation had happened; my very soul had been shaken, and I didn't know what to do about it.

During my coursework at CTS, I took a class on Constructive Theology. It was during this course of study that I was able to name the moral injury that was grinding up my spirit. I chose to study and write a capstone paper on sexual trauma for women in the military. As I delved into this horrific issue, I knew that it would lead me into confronting my own "woundedness" and expose it to the light of day. Suddenly, I found myself careening down a path of self-examination and introspection that I had never thought possible.

Graduates of theological schools often share that they went to the seminary to learn theology and prepare for public ministry. While that is true, what really occurs is that one is transformed in the seminary. Something happens that you never expect and never see coming. For me, it was the realization that war is evil and unjust and that I am a man of peace. But I had participated in a war, and my inner conflict needed to be resolved.

My life put me in contact with other veterans, especially in the American Legion where I rose to the elected position of commander for three consecutive terms. I found in the legion a landing zone of acceptance and an opportunity for leadership on veterans' issues. The camaraderie of former warriors was comforting, but I encountered no one who felt as I did. Our post had members who were combat veterans along with guys like me who did what we were asked. I never engaged in conversation about the morality of what we did in Vietnam. Most encounters were lighthearted, shallow banter about memories of wartime service.

I did come to realize the pecking order among veterans, with combat veterans being the most esteemed even though they were often the most broken. The CIB, or Combat Infantryman Badge, clearly delineates those who have endured ground combat. Soldiers proudly wear this insignia on their uniforms, displaying it for all to see that they are set apart—the elite members of the army. Combat or war-related experiences or questions were relegated to these decorated individuals. Noncombat veterans kept their stories to themselves, unable to compete with those who engaged the enemy in lethal combat. The acronym assigned to those of us in support positions, REMF (rear-echelon motherfuckers), was demeaning and disrespectful.

Shouldering this baggage, I decided to write. The words poured out like a torrential rain, draining my emotions, flooding my life with anger, guilt, and shame. I began to talk about "moral injury," and as I explored my army experience, I began to see how it had affected my soul. It was at this point that I became aware of the role that the church played in my decision making and in the moral code that guided my life. I was raised in a strong, Roman Catholic family where I prayed together with my family every night, attended weekly and often daily Mass at the local Catholic church, and received my primary, secondary, and advanced education in Roman Catholic-affiliated educational institutions. The ethos of the Roman Catholic Church so thoroughly surrounded me that it was no surprise when I felt a call at an early age to ordained ministry.

All these experiences formed me into the man I am today. The journey from "woundedness" to wholeness is ongoing. I have sought healing and forgiveness for the decisions I made as a young man facing the most difficult of choices. It is interesting that the soul-searching and the quest for meaning occurred forty years after my military experience. As the seasons of my life turned over like pages in a novel, I have been driven to address the issues of morality and ethical conduct that I struggled with in my twenties. Writing this memoir has been therapeutic, laying bare my soul for all to see.

I hope this book will be helpful to other veterans who struggle with similar questions. It might assist their family members and friends who would like to gain a better understanding of what their loved ones experienced while serving their country.

INTRODUCTION

I was lost. I had gotten separated from my platoon as we swept through a jungle of elephant grass that obliterated my vision and distorted my sense of direction. The heat was unbearable. I was drenched to the skin, my slippery hand gripping the stock of my M-16 and my helmet anchored on my head, escalating the heat even further. In an instant, I was face-to-face with a small, dark-haired Vietcong guerilla. Clothed in black-silk pajamas, he displayed neither terror nor surprise as his eyes met mine and he raised his AK-47 and pointed it directly at my chest. There was no time to think. No time to react. I screamed, trying to divert the bullet as it exploded at my chest.

"Dick, what's wrong? Wake up. You're dreaming again." My wife, Karen, shook my shoulder trying to bring me back to reality.

"It seemed so real," I said groggily, rousing from my stupor of an

INVISIBLE SCARS *of* WAR

all-too-lifelike portrayal of my past as a grunt, a soldier, a citizen-soldier in Uncle Sam's Army.

Forty years after the Vietnam War ended, dreams like this one didn't come around very often. But this one was especially vivid and traumatic. I wondered, *what was going on with me?* This wasn't the first time I had dreamed of being back in Southeast Asia. Most of the others were about preparing to be deployed or waiting for the trip home and missing my flight.

I was becoming obsessed thinking about my military career, pouring over snapshots of concrete bunkers, lookout towers, and concertina wire that bled out into the lush green rice paddies of Phu Bai, the hamlet where our base camp was situated. My life as a twenty-five-year-old young man had been riddled with internal struggle that had accompanied me for those eleven months I was in-country. I was part of the war machine that churned up the rice paddies, defoliated the jungles, and despised the people of a proud, ancient culture.

It was in Vietnam that I was wounded. I suffered wounds that were not visible to the naked eye. They were internal wounds deep in my soul, and I didn't realize they were there until many years after I had left Vietnam. These wounds of the soul are considered "moral injury," a new term in the military lexicon that includes post-traumatic stress disorder and traumatic brain injury to name a few of the more recognizable maladies. This disorder is difficult to treat and healing is a lifetime endeavor.

> "*Moral injury* has come to mean the transgression, the violation, of what is right, what one has long held to be sacred—a core belief or moral code—and thus wounding or, in the extreme, mortally wounding the psyche, soul, or one's humanity."[1]

---

1   Robert Emmet Meagher, *Killing from the Inside Out* (Eugene: Cascade), 4.

CHAPTER 1

I Am a Patriot

I'm reminded of my time in the army every day. As I'm getting dressed for work, I don my shirt and pants and adjust my gig line, the alignment of the seam of the shirt, belt buckle and trouser fly-seam. The officer at Fort Lewis told me that I'd never forget my military service and I'd adjust my gig line for the rest of my life. I guess he was right. On the wall next to my dresser is a shadow box containing a photo of myself in Vietnam, the medals I earned, my dog tags, and an MPC (Military Payment Certificate) for one dollar. Every day I view these reminders of what I was doing when I was twenty-five years old.

I often wonder, though, why my service in the army haunts me constantly, why it creeps into my thought patterns and affects the things I say and do. I think part of it is that being drafted and serving in a war zone is a unique and terrifying experience. I had never worried for my life, never feared that I was hated for what I was and what I represented.

It felt to me like a seminal event—being prepared to kill an unknown enemy, learning to handle lethal weapons—and wondering whether life would ever return to normal again.

My army life is important because it disrupted my life, put my career aspirations on hold, and shipped me nine thousand miles from home to a part of the earth God had forsaken. It is of utmost importance to me that I don't feel like my time in the military was wasted in a meaningless war that the country was trying to forget and put out of its mind. I don't want to feel like I was a part of something immoral—something that was against my moral code and the values that were important to me as a young man.

I am terribly conflicted over my pride in serving my country and my personal participation in the Vietnam War. I'm a patriot. My heart swells during the playing of John Phillip Sousa marches at football games. I stand at attention during the playing of the national anthem and have led memorial services for years sponsored by my American Legion post. My blood runs red, white, and blue, and I feel privileged to live in the United States of America.

However, as my temples have turned gray, I have begun to question the morality of the participation of the United States in the Vietnam War. And, even more importantly, I now regret that I was a participant in that war. I have equated my role in the war machine to those who were forced into combat, who took human life and did so believing that the soldiers and civilians they killed were inferior, foreigners and less than human. All of us who went to Vietnam played a role in the killing. Although many of us performed noncombat roles, we were all part of the war, and we deserve to bear the guilt and the shame.

I carry this guilt with me trying to rationalize it with the pride of service to my country, and I feel conflicted. I find myself conflicted about wearing my Vietnam Veterans cap, telling the world who I am, that I served during wartime in a combat zone. There is something in me that needs to express that this is an important part of my history. Maybe my reluctance goes back to the early 1970s when I came home, and learned that the country didn't appreciate my personal eleven-month sacrifice. Maybe my reluctance is due to my tour of duty being relatively safe from the battlefields of Khe Sanh and the Laotian border where a number of my buddies were sent. I felt that I would be judged for the role I played in the war.

How can I reconcile accepting words of gratitude for serving in an army that indiscriminately gunned down entire villages of native people, poisoned their farmland and lush forests with defoliants, and abused their women while emasculating their proud fathers and brothers? I crave the adulation of my friends and neighbors who are in awe of what I have done in my life, and I appear to be a strong, well-adjusted survivor. My Vietnam Veteran hat seems to be a common thread throughout these stories. I wear it at times with pride and at other times with the confusion that reflects the sentiment of a troubled soul.

But I grew up watching newsreels of battles during World War II. I cheered for the good-looking, blonde flyboys who bombed Nazi munitions factories and who shot down Japanese Zeros in aerial dogfights in the Pacific. I saw the dogged determination on the faces of infantry soldiers marching through bombed-out cities. I reveled in the parades of liberation where the country came out to cheer the victory that their young men had achieved.

I feel dishonest, playing both sides, unable to reconcile the two positions. What complicates this is the morality that wraps itself around participating in war and about war itself. I studied war and consulted contemporary theologians like Stanley Hauerwas and Walter Wink who influenced my thinking on nonviolence and "just war." Their writings expanded my thoughts, challenging long-held belief systems that formed me as a young man. Instead of providing clarity, I felt more conflicted as I tried to reconcile these new thoughts with the role that religion had played in my life, guiding my moral compass, showing me the path to truth.

CHAPTER 2

Mount Greenwood

M̲ount Greenwood was my neighborhood growing up on Chicago's Southwest Side. Its grid of post-World War II bungalows was planted between three cemeteries and the rich, loamy farmland that would later become Oak Lawn and Evergreen Park. However, to Roman Catholics, it was identified by the name of the Catholic parish that occupied its footprint, St. Christina Church. St. Christina was a melting pot of ethnicity. Originally settled by Lithuanian and Dutch immigrants, the aftermath of war brought in Irish, Polish, Czechs, and Italians. Although their families originally landed in enclaves populating neighborhoods like Bridgeport, Marquette Park, and Gage Park where they attended their own ethnic churches, their kids migrated to Mount Greenwood to build and occupy their first homes, raise their kids, and forget about World War II. St. Christina opened its doors to every refugee who settled in its borders, all except people of color.

African Americans were confined to neighborhoods on the Southeast Side in Bronzeville, Chatham, and Grand Crossing. Even today, racial bigotry is staunchly planted in this blue-collar community of union tradesmen and women, police and firefighters.

The tidy side streets and neatly trimmed bungalows defined the neighborhood that was St. Christina Parish, defiant like a prizefighter looking for his next opponent. The parish church and massive elementary school formed the center of Catholic identity. Staffed by a phalanx of nuns, the Dominican Sisters of Springfield, Illinois, the parochial school provided the indoctrination in the tenets and ethos of Catholicism through daily religious instruction coupled with attendance at weekday Mass, the celebration of the Last Supper of Jesus Christ.

It was in the fifth grade that Father Leo Petkus visited our classroom and invited the boys of the class to study to become *acolytes*, or altar boys, as we were known. My hand shot up like a cannonball. I wanted to serve at the altar. Everything about this opportunity attracted me. The vestments, the liturgy, the elaborate ceremonies coupled with being on the altar with the young priests I admired. It all worked for me. I dove into the booklet on *How to Serve Low Mass* and began memorizing the Latin responses and prayers. It didn't take me long before I was spouting Latin like a Roman orator.

It was not only a sacred privilege to be in the sanctuary, but it allowed me to peer into the life of a priest as he vested in the sacristy and celebrated the Mass. I began to feel that I'd like to be a priest, also. I saw the respect that the public gave to priests and how the teenagers idolized these young men as heroes and role models. As I served at the altar during Sunday and weekday masses, I was selected as the master of ceremonies, a high honor as the only acolyte for this duty. In this capacity, I played a key role in the special liturgies during Lent and at other times in the church year. This key responsibility contributed to my sense of a faint call from God to pursue the priesthood as a lifelong vocation.

Mount Greenwood was an ocean away from the centers of dissent during the late 1960s. Protest marches at the University of Chicago and at the Democratic National Convention in Downtown Chicago in 1968 never reached the perimeter of Mount Greenwood's bastion of blue-collar dwellers. News reports of peace gatherings or civil disobedience simply weren't relevant. Organizers avoided the Southwest Side, and if young men wondered what alternatives they had to avoid military conscription, there were few advisors among the clergy or community leaders. Reports of protest led by activist Roman Catholic priests Daniel and Phillip Berrigan were thought un-American and even Communist inspired. The Berrigans and their movement of training protesters to invade draft boards to destroy records of draft-eligible young men never took root in the working-class neighborhoods of Chicago.

Mount Greenwood formed me as a young boy. My parents built their first house there after migrating from Gage Park, a neighborhood halfway between Midway Airport and the Union Stockyards. My dad was a plumber and worked for my grandfather at his plumbing shop at Talman Avenue and 51st Street. He began his plumbing career after serving in World War II in the South Pacific with the Army Air Force. Dad's outfit built the runways on Saipan and Tinian Islands that our B-29 bombers used to bomb Japan. Mom and Dad married shortly after he returned to the states and I was born a year later. My mother ran our household providing for the care and feeding of the six of us. My siblings included four sisters and my brother.

Our small cape-cod style brick home on the neatly constructed grid that made up Mount Greenwood was a vintage post-war development. My parents occupied the first floor bedroom while my sisters split the two upstairs bedrooms. My brother and I slept in the basement in a remodeled family room turned sleeping space. We were a lower-middle class family in a blue-collar neighborhood full of large families building a future.

I played baseball on the corner of 109th Street and Lawndale Avenue where sewer covers functioned as bases. We batted balls into windows, trampled newly seeded yards, and spent endless summers playing baseball until the calls for supper were heard down the block. In winter, we threw a pigskin, and our passing routes ran us between parked cars to snare lofty passes. As snow packed the unpaved streets, adventurous boys "flipped" cars, hanging onto back bumpers for a ski ride on penny loafers. We sat on porches waiting out the torrid summer void of air-conditioning with our parents draining a Hamm's or Meister Brau. Muscle cars with glass packs lumbered down 109th Street in hot pursuit of feminine intrigue. Life was good on the block. We didn't know any better, and Ike was president.

My life revolved around the block we lived on. Everyone knew everyone else. Even today, I can drive down Lawndale Avenue and name the families that inhabited each home on our block: names like Doherty, Guntorius, Dietrick, Boike, and McHale. They were Germans, Irish, Lithuanians, and Poles who all lived together forming a community. It was a true melting pot of ethnicity and religious traditions spanning the gamut from Dutch Reformed, Methodist, and Lutheran to the predominant Roman Catholic population.

The 19th Ward was a blue-collar, working-class neighborhood bordered by 103rd Street on the north, 115th Street on the south, Mount Greenwood Cemetery on the east, and Pulaski Road on the west. It was settled by young families after World War II who were buying their first home or folks from Englewood who were fearing the encroachment of blacks during the great migration. Former GIs got city jobs as policemen, firemen, or worked for City Hall issuing permits or collecting taxes. A great number of them joined the building trades like my dad, who became a plumber, or Mr. McHale from across the street who worked for the phone company. Others, like Mr. Van, served in World War II and then were recalled to serve in Korea in the early 1950s. They were patriots, surviving the war either in the military or on the home front. They believed in their country and supported it right or wrong.

When US involvement in Vietnam began to escalate, they were torn between supporting their country and safeguarding the lives of their sons and daughters who would be called on to fight yet another overseas war. After World War II, they never thought they would be sending their children to fight in a foreign war. Gradually, many young men enlisted in the marines or the navy while others waited to be called after the military draft was reinstated in 1969 with the first draft lottery. These young men would be "drafted" into the army or the marine corps.

It was a shock for me to hear that one of the kids I grew up with had decided to leave home and defect to Canada. Kenny lived on Ridgeway, across the alley from our house. I heard of his decision to leave the United States to avoid military service and wondered how difficult it must have been for him to say good-bye to his parents. Kenny's dad was a tough, crusty milkman who must have been devastated with his son's decision. Needless to say, the war was responsible for dividing that closely knit family.

Joey, the kid who lived in the one-story bungalow across the street from us, enlisted in the marines in the mid-1960s as the war was ramping up. He served in a combat platoon in Vietnam following in the footsteps of his father. Tom, my best friend in grammar school, served in Vietnam in the army as a forward observer. His small helicopter was shot down by enemy fire but Tom survived, much to the relief of his parents, who were both veterans of World War II. My lifelong friends

Roger and John received deferments because of their teaching profession. I never harbored any resentment toward the two of them, admitting to myself that I wasn't a teacher and couldn't pursue that career path. I learned many years later that the war also tormented them with the choices they had made while watching me getting caught up in the torrent of the war in Southeast Asia. The Vietnam War was not the patriotic cause that our fathers had rushed to the enlistment office to defend. It was a confusing, conflicting, deeply divisive series of choices that plunged our country into a deep morass that would claim more than fifty-eight thousand young people, guys like me and others on the block in Mount Greenwood.

This was the backdrop and early formation process that helped me knit together a code of morality that became ingrained in my soul. Most of the instructions and beliefs were mere words but beliefs nonetheless that would later return with the ferocity of a tornado. These belief systems would question deep issues of moral conscience, issues that would rock the souls of young men like me called upon to defend the liberty their fathers had fought for in the Pacific and European theaters of World War II.

Ora et Labora (Pray and Work)
~Quigley Preparatory Seminary

Ad Majorem Dei Gloriam (To the Greater Glory of God)
~Loyola University

Christo et Ecclesiae (In Christ and the Church)
~Chicago Theological Seminary

CHAPTER 3

College—And Then What?

I walked across the stage of the auditorium theater and accepted my diploma from President James Maguire, S.J., of Loyola University in January, 1969. My parents were there along with all my classmates. Everybody was proud of me. I was, too but the war was lurking in the back of my mind. How long would it be before my number, #178, was called? I was now the most popular commodity in the selective service system, carrying a draft card with a classification of 1-A.

At Loyola, I had finished a degree in psychology in three semesters after I left St. Mary of the Lake Seminary where I had pursued a theological education and ordination to the priesthood in the Roman Catholic Church. Loyola was a soft landing for me where I could parlay the credits I had accumulated studying philosophy and theology; and gain a degree in a related field, all the while enjoying the benefits of a coeducational classroom environment. The curriculum wasn't demanding, and it allowed me to work at the local post office as a letter carrier in my spare time.

Loyola and its student body were timid when it came to addressing issues of social justice and the peace movement. It was a commuter college that achieved the pinnacle of college basketball acclaim when it won the NCAA basketball championship in 1963. After that success, it was largely unknown on the national scene. Its Jesuit-led faculty educated students who couldn't afford Notre Dame or Northwestern University. It was a middle-class family's university with a respectable law school and school of social work. It prepared its graduates for careers in business, nursing, and the social sciences to join the work force in metropolitan Chicago.

Loyola was not a hotbed of political dissent like the esteemed University of Chicago. Students didn't organize sit-ins in the administration offices nor did they boycott classes in protest of the war in Vietnam. There was no organized effort to resist the military draft, no booths in the student union instructing young men how to get deferments or how to pursue other efforts to resist the military draft. Everyone seemed too busy commuting, working part-time, and studying to get involved in the peace movement, attend rallies, and join protest marches.

For me, Loyola was a necessary means to an end of getting a degree. I didn't have the time nor the passion to engage in extracurricular causes and wasn't focused on a particular career path. The draft was paramount in my mind; however, I wanted to graduate, get my military service behind me so that I could get on with my life. I was torn about what to do. I didn't have a career path ahead of me that I was focused on. The war was raging with body counts being broadcast on the Friday evening news. That scared the hell out of me, but I seemed paralyzed in terms of what to do next. Should I join the reserves, apply for conscientious objector status, join the Peace Corps, or defect to Canada? None of these alternatives were attractive to me. I was frozen in place, not knowing where to turn.

CHAPTER 4

A Plumber's Apprentice

Fresh out of alternatives, I asked my dad if I could join him in the plumbing business as an apprentice plumber. I think he was both surprised and pleased that I would follow in his footsteps. Talman Plumbing Company was located on Fifty-First Street and Talman Avenue on the South Side of Chicago. My grandfather had started the business after he returned from the army in World War I. Dad became a plumber after he returned to civilian life after World War II. I think my mom had a lot to do with Dad getting into the plumbing business because she worked in the plumbing shop as a secretary and bookkeeper. I'm sure she asked her father to give Dad a job since he had no career path in mind after the war, and they were married and I was in the picture at that point. After my grandfather's retirement, my dad and uncle formed a partnership and took the reins of Talman Plumbing.

Starting as an apprentice, I would learn the trade over a five-year period, go to trade school, and ultimately get my union card as a licensed journeyman plumber. But before I could begin, I had to be accepted in the union. Talman was a union shop, and joining the union was the path to a job and a career in the trades in the city of Chicago.

Plumber's Hall, home of Local 130, was located on West Washington Street on the West Side of Chicago. My dad and I drove down there one day to meet with Ed Mravic, the business agent of the union. We waited patiently in the cavernous hall until we were summoned. The two of us should have been carrying gold and frankincense to pay homage to this powerful man because he was the gatekeeper. He let you in only if you were the son of a plumber or you had some political connection like working on a political campaign for your alderman or contributing to the reelection of Mayor Richard J. Daley. Minority applicants had a near-impossible time getting in because they didn't have the connections, and there were a lot of Irish, Czechs, and Polish who wanted union jobs ahead of them.

We sat down across from Mravic who was sitting behind a massive mahogany desk filled with papers. "What are you here for?" he bellowed.

My dad answered rather apprehensively, "This is my son, and I'd like him to join the union." I had never seen anyone intimidate my dad before, so this was quite a spectacle.

Suddenly, the monster behind the desk turned toward me and asked, "Do you want to be a plumber?"

"Yes, I answered." That was it. No small talk from any of us.

"OK," he barked like a hungry dog, "you're in."

That was it. The mantel had been passed from father to son. I had feelings neither of excitement nor relief. I was marking time. The military drumbeat was getting louder and would eventually arrive at my front door.

My dad and I thanked him and backed out of his larger-than-life presence. We drove home to the South Side in silence. I had no idea what my dad was thinking, but I knew I wouldn't be an apprentice very long. With a college degree behind me and a draft card stamped 1-A, I knew I'd be in Southeast Asia soon, nine thousand miles from the family plumbing business.

But, in the meantime, I went to work as an apprentice in my dad's plumbing business. It was weird working for my father. I didn't know whether to call him Jim or Dad or Mr. Hattan. So, I didn't call him anything, at least around the shop. Working in the building trades was a welcome change from the classroom, but working outside on construction sites and in dimly lit basements wasn't as exciting as I had imagined. Learning about plumbing was a big change from classroom lectures on ethics, theology, and psychology. The guys I worked with were high school grads and couldn't understand why a guy with a college degree wanted to be a plumber.

New Card Will be Issued Only Upon Return Of This One.

CHICAGO JOURNEYMEN PLUMBERS

APPRENTICE—LOCAL 130, U. A.—BLDG. CONSTR. DIV.

Office: 1340 W. Washington Blvd.   HAymarket 1-1010

THIS IS TO CERTIFY THAT

Richard Hattan

is a member in good standing of above Association. Said order grants his working for quarter ending on date indicated below.

Edward F. Brobec, Sec. and Treas.   Stephen A. Kendricks, Rec. Sec'y.

Dues paid to _June 30, 1970_

278

My apprentice plumber union card.

The apprenticeship program involved classroom study one day a week at Washburn Trade School. In this run-down, converted factory, apprentices learned welding, copper sweating, and lead-piping techniques in addition to classroom work and mechanical drawing. I enjoyed the drawing most of all and began to think that I might be well suited for work as an estimator with a large plumbing company. I didn't care for the work outside in the cold, digging trenches by hand, and doing the actual rough-in plumbing work on muddy construction sites. I had hopes that I would eventually take over the business from my dad and uncle and grow it into a large, profitable plumbing empire.

Unfortunately, the work just didn't click with me. I was very unhappy with it, and it was also during this time that I broke up with my girlfriend of two and a half years. Nothing was going right for me. I sat down with my mom after work one day to talk about my dilemma. She read me like a book and knew I wasn't happy in the plumbing business. When my dad came home from work we all sat around the kitchen table. Dad told me he wanted me to be happy and not to do this just for his sake. He could tell from my listless behavior on the job and my lack of excitement about the business that I had not yet found my place in the sun. I didn't know what to do next, so I decided that I would enter the military when my draft number was called and spend the next two years in the army figuring out my future.

CHAPTER 5

Other Options

Realizing that military service was inevitable, I went shopping, in my mind at least, for the least onerous branch of service. We called it "dodging the draft," but there were legitimate alternatives to the army. I learned about the Naval Air Reserve based at the Glenview Naval Air Base in Glenview, Illinois, about an hour and a half from home. The recruiter was helpful and anxious to welcome me into the navy, so I submitted for a physical and waited to be called for the swearing-in ceremony. I became aware shortly thereafter that naval air reservists were being sent to Nam and assigned to swift boats to patrol the dangerous brown waters of the Mekong River. This knowledge, plus the realization that I would be making a six-year commitment to active duty plus regular monthly meetings and annual encampments, caused me to dismiss the option.

I considered becoming a Peace Corps volunteer, not really knowing anything about it other than what I'd read. The word on the street was that you could serve two years in the Peace Corps and then return to the United States only to be eligible for the draft. So, the Peace Corps was ruled out as a potential deferment option. The Peace Corps was considered by some to be a vehicle to wait out the war hoping for a conclusion to hostilities and an end to the draft. I didn't want to gamble on the United States getting out of the war anytime soon, so that was not for me, either.

Finally, fleeing to Canada was not an option for me. I couldn't face my dad and tell him I was running away. I feared that it would hurt him deeply and cause him to disown me. Where would I go even if I chose that alternative? There was no superhighway to draft freedom available in those days. So I ruled out Canada. I would not refuse to serve and go to jail. That was a certainty. So, I faced the inevitable invitation from Uncle Sam to serve in the US Army. I just sat and waited.

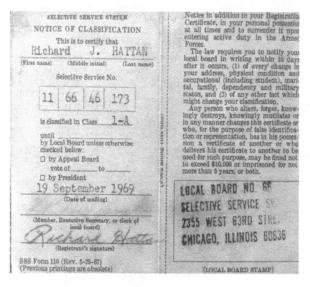

My draft card and my 1-A Classification.

*"The Christian community has never spoken
with one voice regarding war."*

~ROBERT EMMET MEAGHER

CHAPTER 6

Seminary Days

I decided in the seventh grade that I wanted to be a priest. The clergy call wasn't a lightning bolt or sudden sense of certainty, but an answer to which high school I should attend. In Chicago, the Roman Catholic Archdiocese ran a high school seminary, Quigley Preparatory Seminary, a minor league for seminary prospects. I was drawn to the church, attended Mass daily, and served as an acolyte throughout grammar school. When high school arrived, Quigley was a natural for me.

The curriculum was the same as other high schools although more rigorous and demanding, a college prep atmosphere. What was different was the spiritual dimension that was expected though not mandatory. I practiced spiritual reading, getting acquainted with Thomas Merton, Teilhard de Chardin, and Dietrich Bonhoeffer. I began a disciplined prayer life reading the scriptures and learning to meditate. I was introduced to young, active priests who taught our classes.

Although not possessing teaching degrees, these professors, or "profs" as we called them, served as mentors, spiritual directors, and counselors to young men who thought they were being called to a life of service in the church. I was particularly drawn to them because they helped me visualize what I would look like and what life would look like as a priest.

Quigley gave way to St. Mary of the Lake Seminary, its Junior College in Niles, and ultimately the major seminary in Mundelein, Illinois. Academic studies in philosophy and theology were interspersed with social action in the inner city of Chicago. Many of us tutored black children at Ogden Courts Apartments on the near-West Side and visited patients at Cook County Hospital. It was about this time in the late 1960s that the military engagement in Vietnam was heating up. Discussions about the war were academic until some of our former classmates were entering the army and receiving orders to go to Vietnam.

I didn't know what to think about the war at the time. But I do recall that I felt as though my role as a student was without meaning compared to the plight of my friends who were going to war. I didn't think about what it would be like being a participant in the war. It wasn't real, yet; it didn't threaten me at this point, so I looked at military service very academically. I began to wonder why I was resting on my cushy 4-D deferment instead of joining the world and getting involved. This led me to question my vocation to the priesthood and put me on a path that ultimately led me to withdraw from the seminary in the spring of 1966.

I would return to the seminary twenty-five years later, but this time as an Episcopalian at Chicago Theological Seminary (CTS) on the campus of the University of Chicago. The drive to ordained ministry that began in seventh grade had been dormant for many years, but I clearly felt a call to resume my seminary studies and achieve the coveted

Master of Divinity degree. It was different now. I was a senior citizen in a racially and gender-diverse program with loads of life experience behind me.

During a class on the History of American Religions, I volunteered for a class project that would explore the issue of war in recent American history. I covered Vietnam and through the course of the project, I revisited how I felt about the role of the churches in being complicit by declaring neutrality during the war. I also clarified the moral injury that I had incurred by being an active participant through my military service. I wondered why it had taken me so long to arrive at this discovery.

I think that the environment at CTS was what really transformed me. The student body was a mix of gay, straight, black, white, Asian, and transgender students, many of whom found their voices in social activism in the classrooms of Chicago Theological Seminary. The seminary was split in its emphasis, focusing either on black oppression or gender equality. Listening to the plight of my fellow students positioned me into an elite minority group of straight, white males. But, I was a group of one in terms of having survived military service and participation in war. It was out of this context that I felt the freedom to explore the feelings I had repressed about Vietnam.

Many of my professors had been antiwar activists during the 1960s, participating in rallies and engaging in alternate service. They supported me in my quandary now forty years after the war had ended. It was different now. The heat of the antiwar movement was forgotten; the drumbeat of the draft was no longer pursuing me. Now I was looking back, reflecting on the morality of my action and inaction. I had been complicit in an immoral war; there was no doubt in my mind anymore. I needed to find a way to find forgiveness for what I had done, and then to forgive myself in order to be at peace.

The Church of My Childhood

Waves of sweet memories wash across the sanctuary floor,
Where cassock and surplice bore incense-laden boys.
Priests in bright colors chanted in Gregorian verse,
While the choir strained to be heard above the wafting incense.

The answers were easily sung to Baltimore's simple queries,
But lost their meaning in adolescence and first love.
Revolution and Vietnam tore the roots from the soil,
And planted new seeds that grew into free spirits.

The church of my childhood remains a boyhood fantasy,
Of seminary days and Novena-ending vigil lights.
I grew beyond its tentacles and came to believe
That I could never return to its strangling embrace.

Dick Hattan,
Healing Memories

CHAPTER 7

What Does the Church Say?

This short question was the endgame in discussion of faith and morality. Faithful Roman Catholics believed there was some sacred file cabinet lined with position papers on the issues of the day. Parish priests would field these queries from curious and confused parishioners seeking answers to questions not easily answered.

I recall the beginning of my own period of inquisitiveness when a close friend of mine enlisted in the army. Suddenly, I was transfixed by the protest movement, the marches, and the public immolation of draft cards. I attended Mass regularly, even daily, and hoped to hear some indication of the position of the church on the Vietnam War. But the silence was deafening. Many Protestant denominations had issued some statements, taken some position on the war. In fact, the National Council of Churches in 1965 found no justification for continuing the war.

In one of the most publically followed expressions of dissent, Cassius

Clay, aka Muhammad Ali, boxing's heavyweight champion, refused to appear for induction after receiving his draft notice. After being hauled off to jail, Ali was ultimately acquitted of any crime because his Muslim religion expressed a position of nonviolence. Ali had taken a courageous, daring stand against the war claiming he had no hatred for the Vietnamese; the hatred he bore was against white people.

There was no champion for young, white Catholic men. While I couldn't articulate my position at the time, I felt tremendous conflict in my soul trying to follow the example of the nonviolent Jesus I read about in the gospels and between my love of country and desire to please my family and make them proud of their son and brother.

I find it ironic that now, forty years after having served in Vietnam, I learned of the position of the American Bishops of the Roman Catholic Church, dated November 19, 1971, approving a resolution calling for an end to the Indochina War with no further delay. This statement was not without controversy as some bishops interpreted the Catholic position to include protection from participating in this war if one agreed with the Catholic position. For me, this was meaningless. In November of 1971, I had already spent nine months in Vietnam. The American Catholic bishops were out of touch with the people they served. The country had disowned the war, and whatever caused the bishops' reluctance to act showed how truly irrelevant the church had become.

Thoughts about the morality of war continued unabated over the next twenty years as I continued my journey through the seminary. I took a class on ethics at Bethlehem Lutheran Church in St. Charles, Illinois. I was drawn to doing a book review assignment on *Just War Theory*. The book focused on the first Iraq War and George Bush, Sr.'s attempt to justify the war based on *just war theory*. In the course of my presentation to the class on my project, I mentioned that I was a Vietnam veteran drafted into military service in 1970. The professor, a Lutheran pastor, who had spent a considerable amount of time and effort counseling young men about the options that were available other than military service, asked me why I had not sought some alternative service.

I thought to myself, *why had I never met this guy?* The Lutheran Church must have articulated its displeasure with the war and had given their pastors the opportunity to work with young people to avoid military service. What if I had met him back in 1969 or 1970 when I had just graduated from Loyola University? When my draft status suddenly changed from 4-D to 1-A, I was adrift on volatile seas without a friendly port in sight. Maybe meeting a member of the Protestant clergy would have helped me clarify my thinking. Perhaps I could have been introduced to others struggling as I was and would have chosen a different path.

But, I was staunchly Catholic back then, fresh out of St. Mary of the Lake Seminary in Mundelein, Illinois, the major seminary for the Archdiocese of Chicago. It wasn't just the religious influence that weighed heavily on me. It was the mood of the country where dissent was on display nightly on the evening news. My colleagues were on both sides of the war, and it was easy to do nothing and allow the draft notice to step into my life and shuffle me off to Southeast Asia. The hard course would have been to stay home and fight the establishment, to join the marches and attend the meetings planning for civil disobedience. But it wasn't in my DNA. The fabric of my being was knit together in patriotism and the flag. I chose what seemed to be the easier path back in 1970, and the US Army was happy to make room for me.

I wish I had met the Berrigan brothers during that turbulent time. Daniel and Phillip Berrigan were priests who actively protested the Vietnam War. Their nonviolent protest turned into civil disobedience. They recruited converts, indoctrinated them in techniques to help slow the war's advance, and served jail time for their actions. They trained groups to break into government offices to destroy draft records by spilling pig's blood on them or committing acts of arson that had the same effect.

One of the groups, called the Chicago 10, broke into the selective service office at Sixty-Third and Western on the South Side of Chicago on June 3, 1969. My draft board and my records were housed in this office. The band of outlaws set fire to the records of draft-eligible men like me postponing our day of reckoning. I read about it in the *Chicago Tribune* the next day with mixed emotions.

I was happy that I wouldn't be drafted immediately, but regretted that the inevitable had just been delayed. I wanted to get it over with. I didn't know what to do with my life with military service hanging over my head like an iron anvil. Nothing I learned in my collegiate studies offered any interest to me at all. Majoring in psychology was the quickest way for me to get a diploma after my three years of seminary schooling where I majored in philosophy. But I would have rather pumped gas than advance into those fields of endeavor.

Draft #178

It was a number tattooed
on the psyche of a generation,
a symbol of resistance and quiet
resignation, a number that
created an endless supply of bodies
for a shameful nation.

~DICK HATTAN

CHAPTER 8

1-A

I awoke early on the morning of August 10, 1970, the day I was invited to report for induction into the US Army. My letter from the selective service system began with the auspicious salutation, "Greetings." It was a friendly hello but with the strength and venom of the Vietnam War machine behind its kind message of recognition. I had been waiting for this day to occur for over a year, and would have been drafted sooner had the Chicago 10 not set fire to the records at my draft board. Their lawlessness had been temporarily successful since the draft board had to suspend its offer of trips to Southeast Asia in order to repair and reconstruct these valuable documents before the war juggernaut was allowed to rumble ahead once again.

Today was a day I half-dreaded and partially welcomed. It was a sentence I had long anticipated not really knowing its impact on my life and future. I welcomed it because I hated what I was doing, languishing in my dad's plumbing business, knowing I didn't belong where I was, not knowing what to do next. With a 1-A draft classification and an escalating body count in Vietnam, I dreaded where I was going. I was twenty-four years old, college educated, a white kid from a draft board that needed to backfill infantry slots two years after the brutal Tet Offensive.

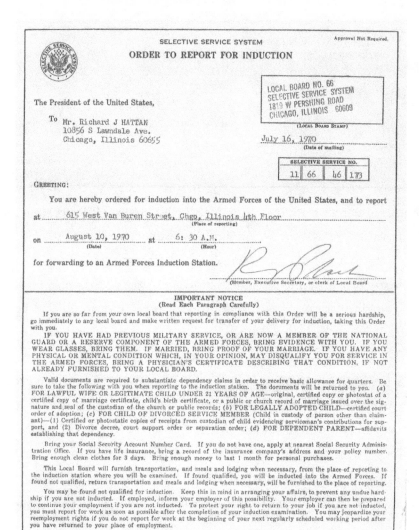

I rode downtown to the selective service office with my neighbor, Billy, another product of the draft lottery of 1969. Billy and I had grown up together on the block in Mount Greenwood. He was a few years younger than me, so we didn't hang around together although we occasionally let Billy play ball with us on the street corner when we needed players to make a game. Billy and I didn't say much to each other during the drive, at least nothing I remember. Billy was hungover from his going-away party from the night before. I had a going-away party, too but it was pretty quiet and reserved. A few of my friends showed up along with my family, but there was no serious drinking that I recall. I just remember feeling scared, not knowing what to expect, and feeling out of my body in some kind of surreal movie. I had the feeling that my family and friends were looking at me for the last time, like viewing a corpse without a casket. I noticed the lengthy glances and felt the extra-long hugs.

Billie's mom, Cora, drove us down to the selective service office early that morning. Cora tried to make conversation with us, but neither of us felt like talking. She nervously prattled on about nothing in particular more concerned about her son going off to war than anything else. I remember driving down the Dan Ryan Expressway early that morning in the middle of rush hour. People were going to work, to school, or off on some errand. It seemed unfair that their lives were continuing on as scheduled while my life was being redirected. I was about to enter the military, not of my choosing, and face the prospect of going to Vietnam to fight and kill enemy soldiers. The lumbering old Ford Fairlane 500 finally arrived at the selective service office on Van Buren Street like a hearse finding a fresh grave. This was it. Reluctantly, we exited the vehicle, said our good-byes, and never turned back.

Then came the first momentous step in my military career. I opened the door to the decrepit office building that served as the army induction center and breathed my last breath of fresh air as a civilian. Inside the door, I was greeted by a red-headed army sergeant who asked me to take a seat and wait for my name to be called. The room was bare of any decorations or pictures. No picture of Uncle Sam saying I want you for the US Army; no army posters of service on some scenic foreign shore; just vanilla-colored walls, creaky wooden floors, and nondescript light fixtures with fluorescent bulbs illuminating the space. Small wooden tables and chairs were ranked side by side in a windowless, open space. Two, five-foot-tall floor fans hummed in tandem moving the hot air around but providing little relief from the rising August heat and humidity. Where was the patriotic music playing in the background? Where were the movies of soldiers rappelling down a steep cliff or parachuting onto a beautifully maintained landing zone? This place was not an enlistment center where young men were personally welcomed by their new best friend, the army enlistment officer. This was serious business.

Suddenly, the red-headed sergeant reappeared and began to bark out names in rapid-fire succession. "Hattan, Richard James." I sprang from my seat and retrieved a large manila folder containing forms and other documents. I would spend the next hour writing and rewriting my name and social security number, an exercise that would sear those nine numbers in my brain forever. I wondered why they needed so much paperwork. At least it diverted my mind for a while so that I wouldn't think about *punji* sticks, booby traps, and Vietcong in black pajamas nine thousand miles away who wanted to send me back home in a body bag.

Now the much-anticipated physical examination would occur. The demeaning process of disrobing down to one's undershorts, waiting like cattle in long lines to incur the cursory examination that would assess my fitness for combat. The comedy of the routine was only outweighed by the sheer lack of dignity of the physical examination itself. We were lined up like cattle being led to the slaughter, told to bend over, drop our shorts and wait for the esteemed physician to walk by examining us from behind. I wondered to myself, *what kind of doctor would perform these inspections? How could they sleep at night knowing they were stamping their approval on all these young men as fit to be thrown into the slaughterhouse?*

With the physical complete and final approval secured, I was herded into an oak-paneled room large enough for around fifty people. The look and feel of this room was quite the opposite of the rest of the building. The American flag was at center stage. Army officers, clad in dress uniforms, welcomed us into the room. This was it. This was the induction ceremony. We swore allegiance to the United States of America and were told to step forward, thereby accepting induction into the US Army.

I thought about my options for a fleeting second. If I refuse to step forward, I'll be sleeping in jail tonight. If I do take this fateful step, I'll be whisked off to basic training where I'll be broken down and reconstructed into a mean, green, fighting machine. I thought about the news clip when Cassius Clay, aka Mohammed Ali, refused to step forward and be inducted into the army. I recalled how he was hustled off to jail when he declared that on religious grounds he could not support or be a party to the scourge of war he would be assigned to help prosecute. Too scared to think any further, I stepped forward and was a soldier.

CHAPTER 9

Basic Training—Fort Dix, New Jersey

Basic training was terrifying! When the transport vehicle dumped a load of one hundred new trainees on the company street of Delta Company, all hell broke loose. Drill sergeants in brown Smokey the Bear hats screamed at hapless recruits. They seemed especially good at finding the bespectacled, uncoordinated, fat guy who had trouble carrying his duffel bag. Inevitably, the poor slob would be penalized with orders to "drop and give me twenty." Observing this in front of me, I lined up with my new buddies and stared straight ahead, fearful to move my head and be meted out the same punishment. This was merely the beginning of the physical intimidation and provocation the army was so good at executing.

It was a surreal time in my life—wearing a uniform every day, not going to work, not going out with my buddies at night. I was learning to be a soldier whether I wanted to or not. I was being trained to kill.

At times, the weaponry I learned to handle and the physical challenges were fun, but at night when I returned to my barracks I would hear the radio blasting the song, "War," relentlessly on WABC. I couldn't get away from it. I was being bombarded with death, violence, and murder every day. The drill sergeants hammered it into our heads constantly that we were going to Nam, going to war, and some of us weren't coming back.

I didn't realize until years later the harm, the moral injury, this indoctrination had on me. I never allowed myself to think about it even though every fiber of my being was telling me that this was not me. I wasn't raised this way. My years of religious upbringing and seminary training were totally antithetical to what I was encountering. The song "War" brought it all home reminding me where I was and where I was going. I was scared shitless.

What came later over the course of twenty weeks of basic and advanced individual training (AIT) was learning the skills to be a grunt, a combat infantry soldier. During this time, the not-so-subtle messages of killing, maiming, and destroying human life were preached alongside the tactical education of survival and self-defense. The songs that we learned while marching contributed to creating a culture of killing and fear. I remember very well marching in formation while singing in repetitive format:

> "I want to be an Airborne Ranger,
> I want to live a life of danger,
> I want to go to Vietnam,
> I want to kill old Charlie Cong."

I hated being forced to sing these words and often refused to join in, but I could see what it was doing to all of us. These words were designed to give us courage to fight and to teach us about an enemy we had never met and knew nothing about. As these songs were drilled deeper and deeper into my psyche, I began to imagine what combat would mean for me.

I can recall the fear palpating through my body wondering how I would react in a firefight, how I could squeeze the trigger of my M-16 as brightly colored tracer rounds bore in on my position. I wondered if I'd become a cold-blooded killer and excel at what I was forced to do. Would my platoon leader recognize my expertise and promote me to "walk point," the lead man in a squad, breaking trail trying to scout the enemy, the Viet Cong (VC) or the North Vietnamese Army (NVA), and engage them in combat? My thinking developed a circular pattern, obsessing, getting nowhere with no one to talk to, not wanting to admit my fears to anyone.

As a divinity student, I was granted a deferment as long as I remained in the seminary. While I never thought my call to the priesthood to be a sure thing, I didn't worry about going to war if I should leave the seminary and pursue secular studies or a career. Guys my age were fighting in the jungles of Vietnam, but it seemed distant to me. While in the seminary, I often sought the counsel and spiritual direction of priests I came to know. Perhaps now I could seek out an army chaplain. Certainly they had experience in helping soldiers deal with the types of issues I was confronting.

After dinner in the mess hall one night, I made an appointment with one of the chaplains on the base, an army captain. The encounter didn't go well. I poured out my feelings that I thought killing was wrong, immoral, and that I was raised a Roman Catholic and had attended the seminary. All I had been taught was telling me that learning to kill was wrong, and I didn't belong here learning to kill.

The captain acted as though he hadn't heard a word I said. He regaled me about how much he liked being around 11Bravos like

me (11Bravo is the Military Occupational Specialty, or MOS, of the
infantry soldier). The MOS is a description of the job one is trained to
undertake in the army. The chaplain talked about how he admired and
liked to be around grunts and passionately told me how he liked how
they lived hard, drank hard, and fought hard.

I knew this was a waste of time and that the army was not interested
in my religious background, my fear of combat, or any other objection
that might surface. They needed bodies in Vietnam, and I would be
sent there whether I liked it or not. I politely thanked the captain for
his time and dejectedly trudged back to my barracks. There was no
place else to go. I don't remember ever feeling as alone as I did then.

Reverend William Mahedy, a chaplain in Vietnam, wrote about the
failure of military chaplains "to discern the moral and religious meaning
of what was taking place. The men, both as soldiers during their combat
and as veterans after the war, have been looking for moral guidance and
spiritual direction, but they have received neither."[1] Mahedy went on to
write that the essential failure of chaplaincy in Vietnam,

> "Was its inability to name the reality for what it was. We should
> have first called it sin, admitted we were in a morally ambiguous
> and religiously tenuous situation, and then gone on to deal with
> the harsh reality of the soldier's life ... in theological terms, war is
> sin. This has nothing to do with whether a particular war is justi-
> fied ... the point is that war as a human enterprise is a matter of
> sin. It is a form of hatred for one's fellow human beings ... and it
> ultimately represents a turning away from God."[2]

---

1   William Mahedy, *Out of the Night: The Spiritual Journey of Vietnam Vets* (New York: Ballantine, 1986) in Robert Emmet Meagher, *Killing from the Inside Out* (Eugene: Cascade), 2.

2   Ibid.

I befriended a number of guys who were college graduates, guys who had been drafted and might be struggling with the morality of what we were being asked to do. There was nobody. I met Jim, a red-headed guy from New York City. We hung around together during our free time playing football and having an occasional beer, but he got sick, was hospitalized, and I never saw him again. He either got a medical discharge or he was cycled back into another basic training company. He may have gone to Nam for all I know.

I wrote home to a few of my friends from the neighborhood but it was futile. They were appalled at the reaction of the army chaplain but they couldn't help me. It must have pained them to see their friend struggling deep in his soul. It was times like these when I felt the growing pains of adulthood smacking me in the face. My parents couldn't help me, neither could my friends. I was now an adult facing tremendously grave issues, and facing them alone.

It was at this moment in time I recognized the gravity of what was happening to me. The training and weaponry were merely exercises up to this point. It was fun competing with other trainees, testing my physical capabilities and endurance. But the reality of what I would be asked to do hit me like a sledge hammer. I was being trained to shed my past, a past that included a loving God; a past that taught me that all people were created equal and that disagreements were settled peacefully. I was being asked, no, *commanded* to kill, to violate the Fifth Commandment, to hate an enemy I had never met and had no reason to murder. All these emotions were flooding my conscious mind making me wonder whether life would ever be the same.

I had hoped to become a chaplain's assistant in the army although I knew in my gut that the sheer likelihood of this would be a stroke of luck. One of my former classmates at St. Mary of the Lake Seminary was a chaplain's assistant at Fort Dix, New Jersey. Fortunately, I was sent to Fort Dix for eight weeks of basic training in the fall of 1970. On a free weekend during basic training, I attempted to look up my former seminarian friend, but I was unsuccessful. A few years later at a party, I was reunited with this individual and discovered that my timing was not in my favor back in 1970. My friend had been discharged from the military when I tried to find him at the post locator. He did tell me that had we connected back then, he would have been able to recruit me to be his replacement. Whether that would have transpired will be forever a mystery.

I met two chaplains during my stint in Vietnam but really had little contact with them. One was a Catholic priest and the other a Lutheran minister. Neither was on the base camp for any length of time except for Sunday services in the Phu Bai Chapel. Chaplains were of interest to me because of my seminary background, but from my conversations with other Vietnam veteran friends of mine, their reputations and my friends' encounters with them only created disappointment and anger.

My friend Alan was on patrol with his unit when a Huey helicopter set down in a landing zone to resupply and deliver a few fresh soldiers to his unit. Among the arrivals was a red-headed Irish chaplain who planned to conduct a service in the field and be airlifted later back to the firebase or base camp where he was stationed. As the chopper touch down in the LZ (landing zone), small-arms fire broke out in the direction of the helicopter. The chopper pilot powered up the bird and took off with the red-headed chaplain on board. The chaplain never touched ground. Apparently, fearing for his personal safety, the chaplain abandoned his ministry to the troops before they had a chance to meet him. Unfortunately, this and other encounters with military chaplains aroused anger among the troops that still has not been resolved to this day.

Chaplains in today's military have contributed little to the debate about the morality of war and the taking of human life. I reviewed a video of a chaplain praying with a group of marine Cobra pilots prior to a combat mission in Iraq. The squadron of young men knelt in prayer as the chaplain prayed for the safety of the pilots and for the success of the mission. I was astounded at the direction that the prayer took. The chaplain was, in effect, praying for the death and destruction of the enemy. It shouldn't have surprised me since I have been aware that military chaplains and chaplains at the military service academies have been dominated by Evangelical Christians who espouse ultraconservative religious positions especially relating to the conduct of killing during war. Meagher states that,

> "The ever-growing influence, even predominance, of Christian evangelicals in the military hierarchy, including the Chaplain Corps, particularly in the Army and Air Force, all but assures the theological and political future and vitality of our national civic religion, with its core belief in predestined American imperialism."

Further, Mahedy writes that the American Church has evaded the dark night of the soul through near total immersion in a culture that seeks personal and national well-being at the expense of every other value.

If the clergy don't provide leadership and critical thought examining the morality of our nation's conduct during war, then where will we find hope for our future? Perhaps it is from those of us who served, who have brought home our wounded souls, who will challenge the American Church to become relevant and prophetic.

CHAPTER 10

Mental Preparation

I can recall the mental preparation that I went through during basic training and advanced individual training (AIT) where drill sergeants pounded me with information, making very sure I knew I was headed for Vietnam and a slot in the infantry. I heard it every day, all day, in lectures, demonstrations, and in physical training and while exercising. It drove me to imagine myself in combat and part of a combat unit on patrol. When firefights inevitably erupted, what would I do? I thought that I'd shoot back either high or low, but off-target. This way I'd be relatively sure that I didn't kill anyone. But what if the lives of my buddies, the other guys in my platoon, came under fire and the only way to save them was to take the lives of the enemy? How would I think my way around that dilemma?

Soldiers in small infantry groups get to know each other extremely well; they must to survive. They know who they can rely on, who the best shot is, and who has the best instincts out on patrol. My insecurity about firing my weapon, about killing the enemy, would surface quickly. I'd be isolated and in more danger than I normally would experience. I dreaded and always had the fear of being fragged or fragging. *Fragging* was throwing a live grenade near one's superior officer or another soldier who was despised for some reason. I didn't want to be in constant fear from the enemy ahead of me and my fellow grunts behind me. So, my thinking process got me nowhere other than getting me depressed and more afraid of the inevitable future that lay ahead.

Still another option was to be assigned to an infantry company but refuse to engage in combat, to defy a direct order. This wasn't a very good alternative, either since it would be considered insubordination, punishable under the Uniform Code of Military Justice (UCMJ). Failure to follow a direct order from a superior officer would lead to imprisonment in a military jail. This was a terrible thought and I easily dismissed it. My future outside the military would be in serious jeopardy with a less-than-honorable discharge and jail time on my record.

I settled on succumbing to the demands of my unit, my buddies, and the US Army training. I would fight, engage the enemy, and suffer the moral and psychological consequences. If I killed in the field, I'd come home and ask forgiveness from God from the priest in confession. After all, I was taught that God forgives even the worst sinners. I didn't think at the time of any moral residual effect of my actions. I didn't think it through that far. It would be a lot worse than I originally thought, but that would come to me later, forty years down the road.

I also didn't think that I'd report to my unit and tell the commanding officer that I wanted to be a C.O., a conscientious objector. That probably wouldn't go well, and I really didn't think I had the courage to go in that direction, anyway. All these thoughts, options, and strategies plagued me through twenty weeks of training at Fort Dix, New Jersey, Fort Polk, Louisiana, and Fort Knox, Kentucky.

CHAPTER 11

Conscientious Objector

Perhaps the world's most highly publicized conscientious objector was Muhammad Ali. Ali received a notice to report for induction at the height of his reign as the World Heavyweight Champion of Boxing. Ali asserted that assuming a combat role would be an affront to his religious and political convictions. Refusing to report for induction, Ali was arrested, stripped of his boxing title, deprived of his passport, and widely condemned for his action. The Supreme Court eventually ruled in Ali's favor, but irreparable damage was done to his career as he faced the prospect of years in jail.

In 1966, the same year Ali became eligible for the military draft, Amnesty International adopted a policy on *conscientious objectors*, people who are eligible for conscription but refused to perform military services for reasons of conscience or profound conviction. Conscientious objectors were considered prisoners of conscience for refusing military service, not for crimes committed, but because of their deeply held religious, political, or moral beliefs.

"It has been said that I have two alternatives," Ali told reporters at the height of the controversy, "either go to jail or go to the army. But I say that there is another alternative. And that alternative is justice."[1]

Basic training opened my eyes to other draftees who were attempting to gain deferments through nontraditional sources. One of the guys in my barracks was a well-spoken black man named John Pepper. John thought that he should have been exempt from military service because of his race. He spoke openly and loudly that he was being discriminated against and that black men like him should be excused. While in basic training, he wrote to his congressmen and pleaded his case to every noncommissioned officer (NCO) he came in contact with. I don't know what happened to him, but I do remember that he was delayed in starting basic training while the rest of us were shuffled off like refugees into an internment camp. My guess is that he found some way out, maybe as a conscientious objector.

I hadn't heard about conscientious objection as a possible means of gaining a deferment from military service until I was at Fort Dix, New Jersey, for basic training. One of my fellow inductees, Jack, was a real leader. He was selected from our group to be a squad leader because of his aggressiveness and athleticism. In fact, he really stood out from the rest of us. After a week or two, I noticed someone else had taken Jack's place in the squad and that Jack was standing off to the side of the formation, hands in his fatigue pockets, with his shoulders rounded and head slumped forward. The energy and aggressiveness were gone. He

---

1   Ashfaq Khalfam, "Muhammad Ali: The World's 'Greatest' Conscientious Objector," *UTC* (June 14, 2016):13:47

was wearing eyeglasses that made him appear weak, and his speech was now soft and dispirited.

When I approached him later, Jack said that he had applied for conscientious objector status, that he realized he couldn't kill anyone, and didn't want to go to Vietnam with the rest of us. When basic training ended in mid-October of 1970, I was assigned to Fort Polk, Louisiana, for AIT. I never saw Jack again.

Fort Polk was known as "Little Vietnam" probably because of the similarity of their climates, which were hot and humid in summer and damp and rainy in winter. The army had simulated the jungles and villages of Vietnam on this sprawling army base, and drill sergeants threatened poorly performing trainees with banishment to tunnel-rat school— whether or not such a school existed I didn't know. As I was being processed into the new camp, I appeared before an officer, 2nd Lieutenant Evans, who checked me in and verified my records. Before I reached Evans's desk, the guy in front of me asked to file for CO status. Speaking haltingly through his tears, this young soldier told the officer that he couldn't kill a fly, he was so passive. Lt. Evans gave him a rough time about it, but he never trained with us, often performing KP, kitchen patrol, or some other demeaning work until his case was addressed. I never saw this guy again, either, until the time I got my orders to report to Oakland for my free ride to Southeast Asia. Being exposed to the plight of the CO, I couldn't imagine myself applying for the deferment. I wrote home to my dad about this young man. My dad's reaction was what I expected from a World War II Army–Air Force veteran. He wrote back saying how proud he was of me for serving my country and not objecting to serve. This just served to add to the heavy load of guilt I felt and the uncertainty of what, if anything, I could do to avoid serving.

I discovered later that the conscientious objector laws protected only those who belonged to pacifist religious traditions like the Mennonites, the Quakers, and the Church of the Brethren.

The Catholic Church, the church of my childhood, was nowhere to be seen on this issue. Instead of protecting its young men in the prime of their lives, it was busy covering up the sins of its pedophile priests and focusing with laser-like precision on the abortion issue.

The Catholic Church was wrong on that issue also, and if not wrong, at least inconsistent. If all life is sacred, why did the church go to the mat on abortion but not on war and especially on an immoral war? The Catholic bishops were out of touch with their people, the actual church, and showed how irrelevant they really were. They had an opportunity to speak out early on the war and protect its young men but chose to hide behind the cloak of power and politics instead of being a prophetic church standing out front against the war.

The church could have made the choice to object to the war much easier for me. It could have laid out a message of morality to our fathers and mothers who fought in a different era, helping them guide their sons and daughters through one of the most difficult times in the history of our nation. But the church chose to be silent and complicit in the war effort when it could have been at the forefront of the peace movement. It could have linked arms with the antiwar protestors and led the marches. It could have opened its massive church doors and held candlelight vigils. It could have remembered us as individual soldiers and prayed for us by name. It could have welcomed us home and provided counseling and reintegration services. But it was silent and did nothing. I can never forgive them for this.

CHAPTER 12

A "Just War": Was the War in Vietnam Just?

M ost Catholics were unaware that it wasn't until the conversion of the Emperor Constantine in 310 AD that the concept of a "just war" became popular. Before 300 AD, many church fathers expressed their opposition to Christians taking up arms. A code emerged late in the fourth century that established minimum moral conditions for the taking up of arms to kill another soldier. It developed once Christians were able to serve in the Imperial Army. The early Christian author Tertullian was one of the first Christian leaders to question whether Christians could ever legitimately shed the blood of others. His answer was quite clear. Referring to the Gospel episode where Jesus was arrested and rebuked Peter for slicing off the ear of the high priest, Tertullian was quoted as asking, "How will a Christian go to war, or for that matter, how will he serve even in peace without a sword that the Lord has taken away?"[1] Tertullian was joined in his aversion to warfare by Hippolytus of Rome who penned a document known as the *Apostolic Tradition*. His writings on military service included the following:

> "A soldier of the civil authority must be taught not to kill men and to refuse to do so if he is commanded, and to refuse to take an oath; if he is unwilling to comply, he must be rejected (by the Christian Church). A military commander or civic magistrate that wears the purple must resign or be rejected (by the church). If a Catechumen or a believer seeks to become a soldier, they must be rejected, for they have despised God."[2]

Simply put, the life of Jesus of Nazareth sets forth a profound and clear message about a doctrine of pacifism. Jesus, a man of peace and forgiveness, never advocated violence, and when confronted with the very real prospect of his own death, asked for forgiveness for those who murdered him. He blessed the peacemakers and preached to love your enemies and to pray for those who persecuted you. This was a message that resonated with my own belief system that actually formed my moral compass and gave it the direction that my soul would follow.

I had been highly critical of the traditions of my former faith tradition while looking for guidance. I had memorized the Ten Commandments, remembering in particular the Fifth Commandment, "Thou Shalt Not Kill." If God had handed this down to Moses, then the church, my church, any church, should have said that it is morally wrong to kill, to engage in war. The silence was deafening. No priest ever spoke against the war from the pulpit, at least not in my church.

---

1   Tertullian, "On Idolatry," 19.318, 321. From *Killing from the Inside Out* by Robert Emmet Meagher. Cascade Books, Eugene, Oregon, 2014.
2   Hippolytus, *Apostolic Tradition*, II.16.17-19.

The clergy that did oppose the war, like the Berrigans, were labeled as cowards and traitors. They were arrested and thrown in jail if they protested and engaged in civil disobedience. And the church remained silent for them, also.

Recently, while searching the archives of the *Washington Post*, I came upon a story that announced that on November 18, 1971, the American Catholic bishops had voted to oppose the Vietnam War since it violated one of the covenants of the just war theory. While hiding behind the tenets of the just war theory, the American Catholic bishops had arrived at a consensus stating that the Vietnam War was immoral. Had I known this back in November of 1971, it wouldn't have made any difference to me. I was in-country, nine months into my tour of duty.

Just war theory is a doctrine of military ethics and tradition often studied in the classroom and on rare occasion by politicians and heads of state to justify waging war. President George HW Bush used just war principles to justify and guide the entry of the United States into the Persian Gulf War in 1990. While going to war should be the strategy of last resort, countries have used just war theory to justify starting wars and as a road map for conducting war once the decision to go to war has been made. While some theologians contend that no war is just, the thought process is helpful in guiding world leaders, academics, and military officials in deciding whether a war is morally valid. The principles that serve as requirements that declare a war just include the following:

- First, the cause must be just. In order to give an affirmative answer to this principle, all peaceful methods including diplomacy and sanctions were tried and failed.
- Second, the intention of the government must be just. The

target nation or faction must be attacking, or a grave and immediate threat must exist that threatens the warring nation.

- Third, the warring nation must represent a valid authority. The
warring government must be valid and follow the rule of law.
- Fourth, only *right means* may be employed in the conduct of
the war. Targeting civilians is prohibited. *Immoral means, such
as chemical warfare,* render the war unjustifiable.
- Fifth, the proposed war must be proportionate to the good that
will be derived. The war must *not* do more harm than good or
may *not* be worse than the cause.
- Sixth, the good to be attained by victory must outweigh the
probable evil effects of the war.
- Seventh, there must be a reasonable hope of victory.

These seven requirements must be met for a war to be considered
"just." Western civilization and Christianity have looked to this theory
in order to consider a war to be justified. If they are not met, a country
could be guilty of war crimes, and in the eyes of Christianity, guilty
of sin.

Three additional conditions must also be met regarding the condi-
tion for the possible conduct of war:

1. Noncombatants must be given immunity and never targeted;
2. Prisoners must be treated humanely;
3. International treaties and conventions must be honored.

Let's examine these conditions to determine if the war in Vietnam
was just.

The Cause Must Be Just. In the war in Vietnam, waging war was
not the action of last resort. There were no peace conferences with rep-
resentatives from Hanoi or the Vietcong. The United States sought to

subvert the government of South Vietnam and antagonized the North through military intimidation that led to armed conflict. Military advisers were sent to aid the South Vietnamese Army instead of an intensification of diplomatic strategies. American political leadership adhered to the Domino Effect, which would result in China spreading its colonial influence throughout Southeast Asia if South Vietnam fell to Hanoi and the Chinese Communist supporters. This principle was not met since all avenues of diplomacy were not attempted, and forms of aggression and colonial imperialism were the main strategies.

The War Must Be Made By a Lawful Authority, a Legitimate Government. The Constitution of the United States stipulates that war can only be declared by Congress and not by the president. The document does provide for the president to act in the event of emergency but not for protracted conflict. There was never a declaration of war by Congress. While the government is indeed legitimate, the president acted unlawfully in exercising the power of war and thus violated this provision of just war theory.

The Intention Must Be Just. It appears that this provision of just war theory was questionable when one considers the expensive commitment to the land bases in Long Binh and Cam Rahn Bay. The intent appeared to indicate a decision by the United States to remain in Southeast Asia for a long time. Such an investment gives the impression of colonial imperialism conducted under the guise of assisting South Vietnam in a civil war against North Vietnam.

The War Must Be the Last Means Possible of Seeking Justice. Clearly, this aspect of just war theory was not considered. Armed conflict was spawned out of guerrilla action and intensified into the devastation of Vietnam. The methods for seeking justice were never attempted. Peace negotiations didn't commence until very late in the war and were never taken seriously by any of the warring participants.

Even organized, nonviolent resistance to the war was never given much attention. The violent intervention of colonization served not to secure a just path to peace but only subverted it further.

Only Right Means May Be Employed. This was one of the clearest violations of the principles of just war. Civilians were targeted by B-52 bombing raids over Hanoi to demoralize the civilian population and thwart the efforts of the military. The use of fragmentation bombs and the spread of defoliants like Agent Orange were used indiscriminately without consideration of the lethal effect on civilians. The destruction of villages, farmland, and cattle was a strategy by the United State and South Vietnam to flush out Vietcong guerrillas but produced hopelessness and homelessness for the citizenry.

There Must Be a Reasonable Hope of Victory. There was never any real hope of victory as all traditional forms of warfare were attempted and failed. Even the bombing of Hanoi failed to bring the North Vietnamese to the conference table for substantive peace talks. There was never a political strategy for the United States, whether it was long-term occupation or withdrawal as a road map to peace. Even a massive invasion was never considered. It makes one wonder at the level of sheer incompetence and misguided stubbornness on behalf of the administration and the highest levels of the military.

The Persian Gulf War, or Operation Desert Storm, was considered by Bush to be just in meeting a number of the criteria for a just war. The potential war should not cause more harm than good and thus be limited in its scope. This war sought to rid the country of Kuwait of the occupying Iraqi army that had invaded Kuwait earlier that same year. Its objective was not to invade Iraq and conquer it but to secure Kuwait and its borders, driving the Iraqi army back into its home country. The scope of the battle involved destroying military targets with minor destruction to civilians and noncombatants. Nuclear or biological weaponry was not used, and entering the war was a last resort after all other types of diplomacy were attempted and failed. Although the Persian Gulf War didn't fit all the criteria perfectly, it was considered by the US government to be a just war.

The Vietnam War could not be considered just; in fact, it violated *all* the principles of just war theory. In the Vietnam War, there were deliberate decisions to bomb civilian targets. B-52 bombers rained bombs over Hanoi daily as an attempt to destroy the morale of the enemy. Hamlets and villages throughout South Vietnam were torched, and jungles were destroyed by napalm in order to flush out Vietcong guerillas and their sympathizers. These actions were not limited in their scope and certainly were excessive, causing lethal harm to the civilian population. The massacre at My Lai was a sad chapter in the war as hundreds of villagers were rounded up and slaughtered in a raid led by Lt. William Calley. These practices were examples of clear violations of just war theory relating to battle after the decision to go to war had been made.

World War II was universally considered a just war, but no church body before or during the war ever examined it in the light of just war theory. John Courtney Murray, the leading Roman Catholic theologian at the time, admitted that no sustained criticism of World War II was made before or after the war by Catholic ethicists.

Many theologians believe that no war is just. I tend to agree. Just war theory serves to offer a way around the teachings of Jesus Christ in the name of nationalism and self-defense. Defending the prosecution of war with just war theory is technically porous and morally weak.

Biblical scholar and theologian Walter Wink wrote extensively on war and peace and stood in opposition to all forms of violence and war. He critiqued just war theory, poking holes in its logic so that the theory deflated especially when we realize how many millions of innocent civilians are killed in war regardless of any attempt to "give noncombatants immunity."[3] Wink actually promoted nonviolence as the way of Jesus Christ. Wink wrote that,

> "Declaring a war just was simply a ruse to rid ourselves of guilt … If we have killed, it is a sin, and only God can forgive us, not a propaganda apparatus that declares our dirty wars just."

Governments and guerilla chiefs are not endowed with the power to absolve us from sin. Only God can do that. And God is not mocked. The whole discussion of just wars is subhuman.[4] Wink thought that the church needed to establish a clear and official position on war, stating that the church opposes violence in all forms. Stanley Hauerwas asserted that there was something in the DNA of Americans that drove them to look to war as the ultimate answer to differences between nations and people. Hauerwas said that,

> "For Americans, war is a necessity to sustain our belief that we are worthy to be recipients of the sacrifices made on our behalf in past wars. Americans are a people born of and in war, and only war can sustain our belief that we are a people set apart."[5]

3   Walter Wink, *The Powers that Be: Theology for a New Millenium* (New York: Doubleday, 1998), 20.
4   Wink, *Engaging the Powers; Discernment and Resistance in a World of Domination* (Fortress Press: Minneapolis, 1992), 225.
5   Stanley Hauerwas, "The End of Just War: Why Christian Realism Requires Nonviolence." In *Clarion: Journal of Spirituality and Justice*, April 26, 2016.

A Catechism of Christian Doctrine
Prepared and Enjoined by Order of
the Third Council of Baltimore

~THE BALTIMORE CATECHISM

CHAPTER 13

Thou Shalt Not Kill

The Sisters of St. Dominic (Springfield Dominicans) taught the children of St. Christina Parish School on Chicago's Southwest Side. During the 1950s, class sizes reached seventy kids in a classroom, well beyond the student-to-teacher ratio that is acceptable today. Families often enrolled all of their children in the local Catholic school, and fathers worked overtime and even second jobs to give their children a coveted Catholic education.

One of the hallmarks of schooling from the sisters was religious education, or catechism class, each day; in fact, it was the first class taught after the bell rang in the morning. The *Baltimore Catechism* was the text each child had in his or her possession. It was written in question-and-answer format meant to be memorized and drilled into the vacant little brains of kids like me, my brother, and my sisters. I can recall participating in competitions that resembled spelling bees where Sister would ask:

Q: "Why did God make you?"

A: "God made me to know Him, love Him, and serve Him in this world and be happy with Him in the next."

I know these answers to this very day. I didn't understand what I was saying half the time, but I was always proud of myself to recite the correct answer and receive Sister's approval.

Another set of doctrine that we learned from the earliest years in grade school were the Ten Commandments. These were statements of belief given to Moses by God on Mount Sinai. They were inscribed on stone tablets and carried around the Middle East for forty years in a gold ark, the Ark of the Covenant. The Commandments found their way into Holy Scripture and were codified and revered by the Jewish people. Eventually, they became doctrine in Christian religions and were to be followed under penalty of sin.

The Fifth Commandment was the shortest, and one would surmise, the easiest to understand. It read, "Thou Shalt Not Kill." Pretty straightforward, right? In Catholic education, we were taught as children that if you violated the Fifth Commandment and killed someone, you had committed one of the most—perhaps *the* most—heinous of all sins. Your soul would go to hell when you died and burn forever with Hitler, Stalin, and Mussolini. That was exclusive of the civil penalties you would also receive, like jail time and even execution.

I never worried about the Fifth Commandment; I never thought I'd kill anybody. As a pre-teen growing up, when I went to confession each Friday or Saturday afternoon, I would examine my conscience and think of all the sins I committed in the past week. Never did I stop and pause at the Fifth commandment; it was never an issue for me. I would frequently go to confession to seek forgiveness for fighting with my sisters or being angry with my brother. I once confessed stealing a one-cent baseball card from my friend's collection. The priest in the confessional must have thought I said that I had stolen a car, not a card, because he wanted to know the make and model! Seriously though, the scope of my disgressions never amounted to anything grave and never got into the serious or mortal sin categories. The nuns did tell us to say three Hail Marys each day for purity. I didn't learn what that was all about until I hit puberty and the sins of the flesh came at me with a vengeance. But I digress.

It was only later in my twenties when I began to think about the war and wonder whether I would be drafted that I thought about the Fifth Commandment. The subject of passivism was not discussed in our schools, not even in our high schools where Catholic children matriculated after eighth-grade graduations. The Catholic high school would become grist for the war's mill where boys who didn't attend college would be listed 1-A and be drafted into the army right after graduation.

Catholic high schools like Quigley Preparatory Seminary, which I attended, continued the tradition of teaching religious education. The life of Jesus Christ was taught. Jesus was known as the man of peace, the Son of God, who forgave his enemies as he died on the cross. There seemed to be a disconnect between the teachings and doctrines of the church, the life of Jesus, and social action that included engaging in war and killing other human beings. There was also a disconnect between the teachings of the life of Jesus and what was discussed at home around the dinner table.

My dad was a wonderful man with strong religious beliefs. He attended daily Mass and received Communion prior to driving his truck to his plumbing shop at 51st Street and Talman Avenue. He was also a

World War II veteran who served in the South Pacific in the army–air force. Dad was typical of men his age who held firm, conservative religious and political beliefs. When confronted with an apparent paradox concerning an action of the president, Dad's response was always that of a career soldier who would routinely declare, "My country, right or wrong" or "He is my commander-in-chief."

I think that my dad was conflicted as events unfolded in the 1960s in Vietnam. He saw the likelihood of his sons being required to serve in an unpopular war for politically and economically nebulous reasons. In order to rationalize the conflict, Dad relied on what he was taught and then moved on, never looking back. I'm sure that the body count broadcast on the evening news was sobering for him, but that the mass protests against the war by long-haired, young draft resisters aroused his ire nonetheless.

So it wasn't surprising that discussion around the kitchen table heated up and often resulted in shouting matches between fathers and sons who looked at the institutions of government, education, and the larger society through very different lenses. The situation in my family was no different. My brother, Gary, frequently locked horns with my dad on a variety of religious and political topics. When my brother came home from high school one afternoon, declaring that Adam and Eve never existed as depicted in Genesis, the first book of the Hebrew Bible, my dad went ballistic. The knowledge and convictions he held dear were under attack and he wasn't about to let a young child of his tell him what to think or believe. I came to understand that my dad and my brother were more alike than they realized which often led them into heated discussions. The Vietnam War drove wedges between fathers and their children during the 1960s, and the absence of any moral direction from the church only served to harden these opposing positions. The silence on the part of the local parish priest or minister echoed the implicit position of the national Christian churches. Absent any direction from the pulpit, families were split on the issues of war and the actions of those involved in the peace movement. Was killing a sin? Was God on our side?

"Thou Shalt Not Kill." Is it a commandment or not? Does patriotism supersede moral values? Is war considered self-defense when it is committed nine thousand miles from home? The church didn't deal with the ambiguity. It vigorously embraced the issue of being pro-life, but that did not include pro-life for the North Vietnamese, the Vietcong, or even their own young men. Terminating the lives of unborn fetuses was being preached against from the pulpit, but the war was never thought to be against church doctrine. I felt that the church was inconsistent in its doctrine of being pro-life by condoning the taking of life in war but opposing the aborting of an unborn fetus.

I recall attending Mass one Sunday after I had returned from Nam. The sermon was presented by a lawyer who spoke about the evil of abortion using graphic slides to horrify the congregation. I was so pissed off at the presentation that I got up in the middle of it and strode out of the church. Meeting the priest in the vestibule, I told him that the church had abandoned me in Vietnam and that the position on abortion was a terrible mistake, inconsistent with the feeble stand it took on war, and was an insult to women. I then said that the church left me in Vietnam, and now I was leaving the church. I've never gone back.

Vietnam was our generation's war. It was an event in time that affected all of us, our entire generation. It signaled the end of governance by our parents' generation, the World War II, so-called Greatest Generation thus christened by Tom Brokaw in his book by the same name. Our public institutions came under criticism, our government and social organizations were all upended. Students engaged in sit-ins occupying administrative offices of colleges and universities. Every available public institution became a site of protest of this war.

While at St. Mary of the Lake Seminary, the Chicago Archdiocese's major seminary, my class learned of the protests at the University of California, Berkeley, and thought, *why couldn't we*? While we didn't protest the war, we did gain our voices and refuse to return to the classroom of professors who treated us like children and refused to share the thought of contemporary philosophers and thinkers. We decided to join the world, overthrowing the curtain of darkness that had been cast over us and regain a position in the secular city.

There was no going back once a line had been crossed, and we found there was support for our subversive activity almost as if the seminary leadership had been waiting for us to awaken from our slumber. The Catholic Church had been shaken from its lethargy by Pope John XXIII through his convening of the Second Vatican Council. I listened avidly to radio broadcasts of plenary sessions and to speeches by Hans Küng and Edward Schillebeeckx, giants in contemporary theology and scholars whose work was not offered in my seminary studies. They encouraged the questioning and the need for reform of an ancient organization that had become covered with cobwebs and grown rusty with skepticism and politics while the poor were entombed in their poverty and the faithful were plagued with an irrelevant, outdated church. The euphoria of John XXIII made way for the entrenchment and regression of Paul VI, John Paul II, and Benedict XVI. The reforms were rolled back, and any thought of further advancement into the twenty-first century was repressed.

Our feeble attempts at exercising dissent on the issues facing the country would not gain firm footing until years later after my departure from the Roman Catholic seminary. Meanwhile, our contemporaries were dying in Southeast Asia, burning their draft cards and worrying about which direction their lives would be taken. But, if you were a divinity student, had some qualifying medical problem, or were lucky enough to have drawn a high number in the draft lottery, you wouldn't have to worry about violating the Fifth Commandment.

CHAPTER 14

An AWOL God

As the Vietnam War marched on into the mid and late 1960s, the church became obsessed with the antiabortion and right-to-life campaigns. The inconsistency of opposing abortion and preaching fearlessly about it from the pulpit was a stark contrast to the silence on a position against the war. Wasn't it odd that the church wouldn't speak out for its youth in the prime years of their lives? I couldn't understand the silence. If priests and bishops were afraid of losing membership by taking a stand for pacifism, they really misread their congregations. People were leaving the church because it was already irrelevant; it already meant nothing. What did they fear? Meagher stated that,

"The church's longstanding obsession with sexuality and complacency with war, still in evidence today, has all but disqualified the clergy and its hierarchy as the church's conscience in matters of making love and making war ... their canonical exclusion from the marriage bed and the battlefield has rendered most Catholic celibate clerics, past and present, personally inexperienced and professionally dubious as moral guides in those turbulent territories."[1]

There must have been a large degree of political muscle applied to the US Catholic bishops by our government. They had to know that if the church came out against the war, that it would have been difficult to fill the quotas of young men during the draft buildup. They could have been heroes! It might have been the biggest political statement of our time. It didn't happen in time, and then when it did occur, the message was weak and lacking unanimity among the bishops. I can't forgive the church for abandoning me. It forced me to do something against my better judgment, antithetical to my own moral code, to do something I was ashamed to support.

It's a fruitless question to ask, but a person of faith must wonder: what kind of God would let war happen? What kind of God would allow the leaders of God's Church to remain silent when they needed to speak? What kind of God would allow children to be harmed by the leaders of the largest Christian Church in the world?

Another myth that permeated the Vietnam War for years and still exists today is that the United States is a nation under God, a Christian nation. Meagher[2] thought that a nation at war is never a nation under God. He also thinks that listening to our veterans may prove to be a conversion experience for the American Church. It is today's veterans who are bringing the greatest clarity to the moral cost of any war. Our

1   Meagher, 131.
2   Ibid. 141.

nation sends its young people to war and claims them as heroes deserving unending adulation and respect. But all too often, these veterans return from war unable to accept the gratitude and respect, and are terribly conflicted with feelings of guilt and shame. Former Senator Bob Kerrey, a navy seal in Vietnam, confessed that,

> "I thought dying for your country was the worst thing that could happen to you, and I don't think it is. I think killing for your country can be a lot worse. Because that's the memory that haunts."[3]

Maybe the questions are too simple. We tend to blame God when tragedy occurs or evil triumphs. Why not? Is God only around during the good times? If God weeps seeing God's Creation killing, brutalizing, and maiming each other, then how much sorrow must God feel about the abuse of children at the hands of Catholic priests? How could a good God allow this to happen? How could God be present and do nothing? How does God let the murders and atrocities occur and stand by, helpless? I, like many of my fellow soldiers, felt that God was AWOL in Vietnam. I wrote this poem to sum up my frustration on this matter:

---

3   Ibid. 143.

An AWOL God[4]

Where were You at the lottery of unsought soldiers
When celebrations and despair spared no youthful face?
Where were You as the typewritten commands
Sent jungle-clad children on missions of murder?

But the Lord was not in the wind.[5]

Where were You when sappers and *punji* sticks
Destroyed limbs of all-American hope?
Where were You as protesting playmates decried the horror,
During the yearlong sentence of death?

But the Lord was not in the earthquake.[6]

Where were You as the spray of orange poison
Rained from heaven with cancerous consequences?
Where were You as the newly armed warrior
Spent a magazine of fire at unseen enemies?

But the Lord was not in the fire.[7]

Where were You during the rape of black silk daughters,
Begging for life during the respite from combat?
Where were You when the war birds' noise
Muffled Your small, still voice?

Were You there? Did you hear me?

---

4   Dick Hattan, "An AWOL God," unpublished poem, 2011.
5   1 Kings 19:11 (New Revised Standard Version).
6   Ibid.
7   1 Kings 19:12 (New Revised Standard Version).

God wasn't there for me in the person of my church to help me avoid participating in this war. God wasn't there for the thousands of soldiers, fifty-eight thousand plus, who lost their lives as well as for the many countless South Vietnamese and North Vietnamese soldiers who also lost theirs, nor for the civilians who were killed fighting for their homeland. God wasn't there for the hundreds of thousands of us who were sent to Vietnam against our will and who survived and returned with lifelong physical and moral injuries. Where were the prophets? Bobby Kennedy and Dr. King were slain and martyred for their outspoken positions on civil rights. They spoke out eloquently against the war but neither were granted the time on this earth to carry out their gospels of peace. If Bobby and Dr. King were prophets, they suffered the fate of their predecessors from the Hebrew Bible who were silenced and denounced for their message. I kept thinking to myself, *when will the church take seriously the Commandment not to kill?*

Mainstream Protestant bodies such as Methodists, Presbyterians, American Baptists, and the United Church of Christ had been officially and mildly critical of the war policy, frequently using the National Council of Churches to express opposition or misgivings about the war. However, some church bodies like the eleven-million-member Southern Baptist Convention, the largest body in American Protestantism, were silent on the war. These churches expressed neutrality but in effect supported government policy. They typically prayed for divine protection for American soldiers, the defeat of Communism, and world peace by extolling the virtues of obedience to civil authority.

Maybe the greatest tragedy of the Vietnam War was the way in which the churches and society in general failed those of us returning from Southeast Asia. We were denounced from the pulpit, referred to as baby killers, and as having committed war atrocities. I never had a welcome home party, neither from my family nor from my church community. While I was in Vietnam, my church never prayed for me as an individual. They did pray weekly for a civilian who was a POW, but the guys in the military were never mentioned. Our church had no psychological or pastoral care for veterans who had experienced post-traumatic stress syndrome (PTSD). No effort was made by the Catholic Church nor any other major denomination to minister to the needs of the men and women who served in Vietnam and help them adjust to civilian life.

A shining light among church leaders was Dr. King in his address entitled, "Declaration of Independence from the War in Vietnam."[8] The address was given at the Riverside Church, New York City, on April 4, 1967, at a meeting of Clergy and Laymen Concerned about Vietnam. In this speech, King suggested five concrete actions for the United States:

1. End all bombing in North and South Vietnam;
2. Declare a unilateral cease–fire.
3. Curtail military buildup in Thailand that threatened other parts of Southeast Asia;
4. Include the National Liberation Front as a player in peace negotiations;
5. Set a date for withdrawal of foreign troops from Vietnam.

He also encouraged all clergy of draft age to give up their ministerial deferments and seek status as conscientious objectors.

All of this caused me great confusion in the 1960s. I had difficulty making decisions about my future, and the decision I did make was the decision to do nothing. It was a decision to let the draft lottery claim

---

8 *The Essential Writings and Speeches of Martin Luther King Jr.*, edited by James M. Washington (New York: Harper, 1986), 231-244.

my number and in due time send me a letter requesting my presence in the United States Army. Not deciding was a lot like being back in the seminary. If you did nothing, the system moved you along and you accepted your fate. So, I did nothing and received my draft notice to report to the selective service system office on August 10, 1970.

I wrote a poem memorializing my draft number and the emotions that these digits evoked in me back in 1969-1970:

178

It was a number unadorned
Without meaning as random digits
Until a fatal game of chance
Ordered lives, prioritized death
Continents apart from life on the block.

Overnight a nightmare disturbed
Sleep and dreams, delaying plans
With months of interruption
Learning skills of destruction and
Hatred of a people unaware for
A cause misunderstood.

It was a number, a conversation starter,
Three digits that would
Land on a date that
Halted a career
Cleansed the present or avoid the
Heartache and loss ahead.

It was a number that by
Delayed reality suspending

Life until it called by
An official letter commanding
My presence, changing my life
Thrusting me into adulthood.

A number not to be forgotten
Disturbing the spirit
Injuring the moral code
Carefully nurtured by parents
And teachers, tearing apart the temple
Veil of innocence.

It was a number tattooed
On the psyche of a generation
A symbol of resistance and
Quiet resignation, a number that
Created an endless
Supply of bodies for a shameless nation.[9]

---

9   Dick Hattan, "178" (unpublished poem, 2014).

Chapter 15

Phu Bai

February 25, 1971

Dear Dad:

I wanted to write as soon as I got settled over here and tell you I was OK. It took a few days to get out of Oakland but I'm here now, half-way around the world, 9,000 miles from home. Some of the guys got diverted to Germany at the last second. You should have heard the cheering that went up when they boarded their bus to fly to Europe. It made the rest of us feel pretty bad since we knew we were going to war, to Vietnam and the unknown jungle of Southeast Asia. On the day we left, a bus took us to a remote Air Force base where we boarded a passenger jet. Everyone was dressed in jungle fatigues, light, comfortable uniforms with lots of pockets, pockets that will later hold magazines loaded with bullets for our M-16s. I rode next to my buddy, Tim, who went through Basic and AIT with me.

Tim is from a small town in Pennsylvania. He's engaged to be married and he and I have become good friends.

The trip over here took twenty-three hours with stops in Hawaii and Japan for refueling and crew changes. It was early morning when we began our approach to Tan Son Nhut Air Base in Long Binh. The plane went into a very steep descent that caused me to experience extreme and painful pressure on my ear drums. The pain was excruciating but I soon realized that a gradual descent on our approach might have been dangerous. We finally landed and taxied to the hanger. When the cabin door was opened, a wave of tropical heat rushed into the cabin accompanied by the smell of rotting garbage. Welcome to Vietnam! The clock had begun ticking for my year-long tour of duty in Vietnam.

As I emerged from the plane, I stepped on the portable rolling stairway that would take me back to earth. My eyes darted surveying the olive drab hangar that would beckon us in our fresh green jungle fatigues into its gaping expanse of space. We were guided along the tarmac by guys just like us carrying fully-loaded M-16s at the ready. I felt important, like precious cargo that needed an armed escort but in reality I was another grunt who would eventually fill in for someone else. This was Asia, a different continent; Vietnam, a country I had never heard about when I was growing up.

I noticed thin, wiry Vietnamese men and women scurrying around with flip-flops slapping on the concrete with lampshades on their heads, clothed in black silk clothing. The war had just become a reality. I was no longer on the block back home and I wasn't going home for another twelve months. This place looks scary and I'm wondering what I'm doing here.

Dick

I got lucky. When I arrived at the 101st Airborne Division Head-quarters to be assigned to an infantry unit, the buzz in the air was that the division was experiencing a shortage of clerks to work in the division headquarters. I was given a typing test because of my advanced educa-tion and test scores and became a REMF that day. I hated the moniker but at the time I was so relieved at my good fortune that I didn't mind being referred to as a REMF, a "rear-echelon motherfucker." The title was new to me when I arrived in Vietnam; it had never been mentioned in my twenty weeks of training. But when I arrived in-country, it became something I coveted. It was a job in the rear, a support position, a military specialty not engaged in combat. Assigned to the 2nd Battal-ion 502nd Infantry, I would be working in the 101st Admin Company in a clerical position typing Morning Reports. Morning Reports were a daily accounting of troop strength in the division. I kept track of troops killed in action, on R&R, and discharged to another assignment. It was painless, and I thanked God for the break.

My buddy Tim, from Pennsylvania, went to the 5thth Mechanized Division in Quang Tri. Tim and I had been drawn to one another in basic training at Fort Dix. We were inducted on the same day, me in Chicago and Tim in rural Pennsylvania where he lived among the Amish. We were both sent to Fort Polk, Louisiana, for AIT and had spent what little free time we had together. We both were religious but argued from different sides of the religious spectrum. Tim believed in the Bible's strict interpretation and I didn't. We didn't see eye to eye, but we learned to respect one another and learn from our differences.

On the night before we flew out of Oakland for our assignment in Vietnam, we wandered into a bar where I drank too much to drown my sorrow, while Tim sat there drinking a coke enjoying our com-panionship. We sat together on the plane hopscotching our way from Oakland to Honolulu to Japan to Long Binh. I don't remember a thing we talked about, but I know we shared the same fear of the unknown that awaited us. After a few days waiting for transport to our permanent assignments, Tim was sent to the 5th Mechanized Division and I was assigned to the 101st Airborne Division. It was the infantry for both of us. We parted wishing each other well and wondering if this were the last time we'd get together.

One day three months later, one of the guys who trained with us in Basic and AIT stopped by to tell me that Tim had been wounded while on patrol in Quang Tri. He and another grunt had tripped one of our own claymore mines blowing off Tim's legs and destroying his hearing in one ear. Suddenly I felt like I was going to vomit; I couldn't believe what I was hearing.

When I left the service, I traveled to Pennsylvania to visit Tim in a VA hospital near his hometown. I was shocked at how different he looked lying there on his hospital bed with his legs amputated. I couldn't believe how small he looked for a guy who was six feet tall. Tim sent me a postcard at Christmas that year writing that his fiancé couldn't handle his injury and had left him; however, he later married his rehab nurse, was managing very well on his prosthetic legs, and was promoted to vice president of the local bank.

Another army buddy, Larry, went to Chu Lai with the Americal Division. Larry humped the bush for a while and then negotiated a job as the company clerk in his unit. I had gotten to know Larry in AIT since we shared the same bunk. We spent a lot of time together during training exercises and afterward in the evenings and when we had other down time.

Once on a twenty-four-hour pass, a bunch of us from our company took a bus to Alexandria, Louisiana, just to get off the base and have some fun. Our group of ten guys included one of our fellow trainees who happened to be African American. We all strolled into a local bar and ordered beers expecting to spend the evening in the establishment. The bartender quickly told us that blacks were not allowed in his bar. Then, without any further discussion or consultation, we all got up and walked out of the bar together. None of us could believe that prejudice like this was still rampant, but what we didn't realize was that we were in the South and it had not yet become enlightened about race relations.

The group found other places to drink but after a few hours of carousing, I headed back to the motel room we had booked. Larry returned much later, pretty inebriated. When he came back in the room, he woke me up and told me that he had decided to ask his girlfriend to marry him. He was totally serious and wanted to call her immediately. I talked him off the ledge and made him agree to wait until morning. The next day, I listened in on Larry's telephone proposal to his fiancé prompting him to tell her that he loved her.

The three divisions, the 101st Airborne, the American, and 5th Mechanized Divisions took most guys who served in-country with me. The guys I served with lucked out the same way as I did (that is, they also became REMFs). We spoke often during our free time of how lucky we were not to be sleeping in the jungle, not humping the seventy-pound rucksack, and not facing combat.

War touched us in a lot of different ways and not just those of us who humped the boonies and experienced the horrors of combat. My buddy, Cliff, was also assigned to the Morning Reports section of the 101st Admin Company but was a member of the 327th Engineering Battalion. One day we got notice that a chinook helicopter ferrying thirty engineers was shot down, killing all thirty guys on board. Cliff had to document and record the names of each one of those Killed in Action (KIA). He was disturbed by it even though he didn't know them personally. He felt the pain and loss that this incident caused and was visibly moved when he related the task he had to do as his part of the war effort.

I never really thought I was out of danger, though. On guard duty defending the perimeter of the base camp, there was always a nagging fear that the sky would light up and a regiment of NVA or VC would come charging through the rice paddies. Mortar rounds occasionally landed in our camp, and "sappers" would sneak through the concertina wire to blow up our ammo dump, but I didn't live through any firefights. Sappers were elite NVA or VC soldiers who were known to approach army base camps and infiltrate the perimeter defense. The only thing I really feared was getting my throat slit by a black-pajama-clad Vietcong who had slipped through the wire at night while I slept on my cot.

We never talked about the consequences of killing. The guys I knew didn't think that deeply or at least didn't have the ability to express their thoughts on this weighty subject. We were all in our early to mid-twenties and didn't have a lot of life to reflect upon. We didn't care about the Vietnamese people and the devastation that the war was inflicting on their land and their culture. There was no thought about what it would feel like to point a rifle at someone, squeeze the trigger, and watch that person fall over dead.

We never saw the grief that war was costing the native Vietnamese people in terms of loss of life and property. Perhaps if we saw the war "up close and personal," we would have discussed the implications. But, there was no emotion, no concern, no empathy for the Vietnamese. In our minds, they were the cause and the reason we were in and had been sent to their country in the first place, and we hated being there. We had conversations about "walking point," the first soldier or most exposed person in a military formation, wading into elephant grass, and searching for trip wires that would detonate mines and other explosive devices. But we didn't feel comfortable expressing any misgivings we might have had about killing enemy soldiers. I know I didn't feel comfortable, and I didn't know any of my buddies I could share my fears with. The NVA and the Vietcong were faceless unknowns to us. The VC could have been employed on our base emptying garbage or doing other unsavory jobs our guys wouldn't do,

When I got home and was discharged from the army, I didn't want to talk about what my job was, and I still don't like to answer the question. First, the most frequently asked question was, "did you kill anyone?" Secondly, those questioning me never really cared about me and what it was like being in a war zone. They wanted to hear the sensational, about blood and guts. I feared being sloughed aside if my non-combatant status was disclosed. One person I knew well tossed aside the danger I experienced by flippantly saying that had I typed my way through Vietnam. This really angered me, and I let loose on him that he knew nothing about what I had experienced and had never asked me about it. The memory of this encounter still enrages me. Over the years, I've downplayed my military career when asked about it because I felt that the only guys whose service was really respected were those who had been in combat.

I found acceptance and comfort by joining the American Legion. I had always thought that Vietnam veterans weren't welcome at American Legion and VFW posts, so I avoided joining. As sentiment changed toward veterans in general, I found the camaraderie in the Legion an unexpected oasis of acceptance. I joined the color guard, marched in hometown parades, and even worked my way up to the elected office of commander. There was no judgment, no uncomfortable questions asked, just a landing zone for anyone who had served.

But the internal struggles of my past didn't leave me. I still hesitate to wear my veteran's cap and am sensitive about the Vietnam Veteran license plate on my car. I wonder if I'm being dishonest proclaiming my service so publicly yet feeling the guilt that I was not true to my beliefs. The wall in my office depicts a shadow box of my medals and ribbons earned in Vietnam. I display them with the pride of having survived my assignment in Vietnam rather than with any sense of patriotic fervor or military accomplishment.

CHAPTER 16

The Phu Bai Chapel

Amid the tedium of life in Vietnam in 1971, there was a shaft of light that brightened my life each Sunday morning. God arrived in Phu Bai for two chapel services, a Protestant service and a Catholic Mass. Chaplains from each denomination conducted the gatherings in the small chapel, which was a transformed hootch, two units away from my abode. The chapel became a source of comfort and respite from thinking about war, about the army, and surviving the sweltering heat and humidity of Vietnam. It was identified by a small wooden steeple with a cross attached to its pinnacle. The doors swung wide on Sunday mornings but remained under lock and key during the week. Its footprint was similar to the other hootches that dotted the pockmarked, muddy street it sat on and held about fifty worshipers on a busy Sunday. A small, wooden altar was centered in the front of the worship space flanked by a small electric organ that my friend and chaplain's assistant, Larry, played with all the gusto the little instrument could muster.

The priest, Father John, called us the "singing chapel" because of the strong vocals that accompanied the sweet organ tunes. The services were a welcoming and uplifting departure from the work of war that we engaged in seven days a week. I recall a sermon Father John preached one Sunday where he called us out for spreading vicious rumors about the soldier permanently assigned to bunker guard atop the fifty-foot-high tower that overlooked our segment of the base perimeter. Word had spread that a number of guys were sexually assaulted, and this soldier was blamed for the offenses. John's strong message was appropriately delivered and seemed to diminish and dissipate the character assassination that had run rampant in the camp. The chaplain saw a wrong being propagated, and he quickly and decisively excised the issue.

I found my life as a soldier in Vietnam to be godless were it not for the Phu Bai Chapel. I went to chapel services every Sunday, but it was mainly to get away for a while, sing some familiar hymns, and pray, though not really knowing for what I was asking. No, God was not dead as some theologians had contended in the 1960s; God was AWOL. I felt abandoned and neglected by a God that had been so much a part of my life as a seminarian, where my day was ordered by prayer and where I had felt a divine presence in my life as a young man.

If it hadn't been for the open chapel door on Sunday morning, I wouldn't have thought about God at all. I never experienced the terror of combat, so I can't relate when I heard it said that there are no atheists in foxholes. The chapel, its services, and the chaplains gave me the opportunity to stay in touch with the familiar symbols and signs of the faith I was raised to know and love. Although God seemed AWOL most of the time, on Sunday morning, God's presence stalked the wooden floors of this simple space bringing comfort and hope through the prayers and hymns so familiar to all of us.

I wonder what happened to this little chapel across from the Repo Depot—as we referred to the orientation area where the FNGs (Fucking New Guys) arrived. I hope its doors continued to swing open for the guys left to defend the base after we left. Later, when the base fell to the advance of the North Vietnamese Army, the chapel was probably bulldozed along with the rest of the wooden structures that housed the headquarters of the 101st Airborne Division. Though I didn't feel it much then, I know now that God was with us during those turbulent times as we gathered to sing the familiar verses that brought a slice of home to Vietnam in 1971.

Eleven months in Vietnam brought moments of levity and joy in the midst of the boring, grinding days of war. While reading letters I had sent to my friend John, I rediscovered a worship service booklet of an ecumenical Thanksgiving Day worship service.

The cover of the ecumenical Thanksgiving service booklet, Vietnam 1971.

The program for the Thanksgiving service, Vietnam 1971.

The Army chaplain organized the service with a special musical presentation by children from the Nhan Duc School. I was asked to participate, reciting the litany of Thanksgiving. I had written on the back of the leaflet a letter that this was something I would always remember.

The memory of Thanksgiving in Vietnam 1971 has faded just like most of my time in Southeast Asia. What I do recall was that it was a free day, no work. We could forget we were soldiers although the green jungle fatigues gave us away. Actually, it would have been weird to see anyone not dressed in olive-drab uniforms. We were a sea of green.

The kids who were our guests at the service were cute and climbed all over us, starved for attention and love. They spoke no English and we spoke no Vietnamese, but we communicated nonetheless by reciting numbers. I knew *một, hai, ba* from the French, so I got the kids to recite the Vietnamese numbers opposite their English counterparts from one to ten. One little kid was drawn to my watch, a black, plastic timepiece with hands coated in phosphorescent paint so you could tell the time in the dark. I took it off and let the kid play with it. I felt sad for these kids, homeless and parentless. I wonder how they have spent their lives forty-six years later, now in their fifties. Perhaps the new Vietnam has been good to them and they've prospered and did not have to live the same meagre life that their parents had experienced in tin-plated huts, selling food alongside the road. Maybe these kids embraced the unification of the country after we left. They might have become the backbone of the new economy, producing goods in factories for the rest of the world. Maybe they're part of the tourism trade and work in resorts on the South China Sea in Cam Rahn Bay, Na Trang, and Hue.

There is redemption here. Good has risen out of a bleak situation. From what I've observed, I'm confident that these children, now adults and perhaps with children of their own, live in improved conditions. Hopefully, prostitution has given way to prosperity and killing has converted to commerce. The children we entertained on Thanksgiving Day 1971 now live a good life, have raised their own families, and have a lot to be thankful about. At least that is what I hope.

CHAPTER 17

My New Block

I stumbled across a photo of the company street that I lived on back in 1971 in Phu Bai.

The Company Street in Camp Campbell, Phu Bai, 1971.

It was quite a change from the old neighborhood of bungalows, cape-cod and Georgian style homes that lined the streets of Mount Greenwood. Hootches lined the dust-covered road; they are wooden structures with an A-line design that have plywood walls, metal roofs, and a strip of screening that covered the openings under the eaves to allow air to filter through. The buildings sat on wooden pylons raised a foot above the ground so the rats could find a home and we could be protected from the weather and monsoon rains.

Each of the six guys assigned to our hootch tried to personalize his space and create a bit of privacy with blankets, poncho liners, and scrap wood. For example, George had a flag of the state of Illinois since he hailed from Mendota in Western Illinois. Rome posted the Buffalo flag representing the state of Wyoming. Doug flew the state of Michigan flag, while Roy and Calvert left their space simple and unremarkable.

I found some scrap lumber and built a writing desk and chair and covered the desktop with an army issue olive-drab towel. I squared off my space by positioning my cot so that it looked like I had some privacy with my mosquito net hanging over my bed. It wasn't much, but it beat sleeping on the ground, curled up in a poncho liner on overnight patrol. The six of us jointly owned a two-cubic-foot refrigerator that had trouble keeping up in the intense heat and almost never created ice cubes. We built a bar in the middle of the hootch that provided a focal point for discussions in the evening.

Down the street was the chapel and across from our hootch was the shower facility and water-pumping station. It was here that orange-colored water provided cool relief in the high humidity of South-east Asia. The water didn't always run but when it did, even the slow trickle of water was a welcome balm. The hootch was home for eleven months and we were family. We sat around the bar at night telling stories of home, getting to know foreign places like Kaycee, Wyoming;

Muskegon, Michigan; Pittsburgh, Pennsylvania; rural North Dakota; Muskogee, Oklahoma; and Mendota, Illinois. We were a melting pot of American young men caught in the military draft of 1970 doing what we were asked to do.

The hootch sheltered us during a typhoon that lashed out from the South China Sea and provided relief from the unbearable heat and jungle-style humidity that assaulted us when we were in monsoon season. It provided private space where we read letters from home and crafted messages back to our loved ones worried about our safety, praying for our return.

I used to write a lot of letters while in the service. I wrote to my family and to several of my buddies back home. It was always a thrill at mail call each day to get letters from "the world" as we called it and to read and reread them in the privacy of my bunk at night. But there was nothing quite like hearing a voice from home, listening to someone talking to you even though they were nine thousand miles away. I was able to enjoy this communication through my combination portable radio/cassette tape deck that I bought in Vietnam at the PX. It must have cost me $50, but the hours of speaking and listening that it provided me were priceless.

Cassettes traveled free through the US mail just like first-class letters. It was a glorious day when a cassette arrived from home. My cassette deck had a small handheld microphone that I'd use that provided pretty good sound quality. The real-time communication we enjoy now through Skype and FaceTime was foreign to the weeks and weeks of delay that I would endure waiting to hear a response from my most-recent recordings. Today, soldiers in the Middle East wars can speak and view live pictures of their loved ones, a benefit we lacked; however, I'm not sure that the immediacy is more comforting or more disturbing. Our need to know doesn't seem to be diminished as our hunger for information and communication continues to escalate.

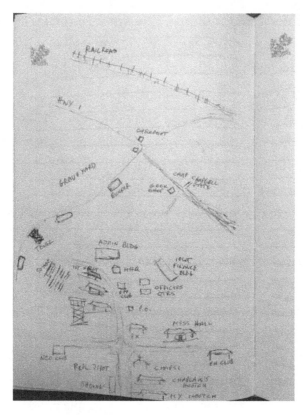

101st Admin Company, Area of Operations.

A road intersected the company street just past the chapel. Taking a right turn led one past the Enlisted Men's Club, a bar run by local Vietnamese workers where warm beer was served nightly. The Mess Hall, dry cleaner, and tailor shop followed as you wound your way down the sand-covered street. The road eventually wound its way to the main gate and emptied out onto Highway 1, the road that reached down the length of the country all the way to Saigon.

The Mess Hall was a clean, orderly place to dine where row upon row of wooden tables and chairs provided a friendly respite from work. The only problem was the food. When there was food, it wasn't bad; but, the selection was poor with stewed tomatoes and lima beans featured nightly accompanying the main entrée. Most of us stopped eating there or only ate one meal a day. The word around the camp was that the supply sergeant was on the take and sold the good food to the black-market thus bypassing most of the troops. Some of the recipients of this illegal generosity were my fellow soldiers. I often noticed steaks being grilled behind many of the hootches, food that never made it to the Mess Hall.

When I did darken the door of the Mess Hall, I did so to take my weekly malaria pill. We were all "on the pill" and survived that dreaded disease since sanitation was poor and disease could have run rampant through our compound.

Returning to my description of the company street, our PX stood at the crossroad, the center of our compound. It was a tiny shack that had very little merchandise, mainly soap, shaving cream, and an occasional candy bar. This was nothing like the PXs in Long Binh on the sprawling army base adjoining Saigon. At Long Binh, you could buy refrigerators, jewelry, and Rolex watches in their air-conditioned PXs that played soft music. There were snack bars where you could buy hamburgers, chocolate milk, malts, and cherry cokes. Clearly, there were vast differences in the face of the war depending on where you were stationed.

Continuing on along my street, there was a post office shack next to the PX, a very popular place during the daily mail call. It adjoined the officer's compound, a little slice of heaven nestled between the sparsely appointed hootches used by the enlisted men and the nicely decorated, air-conditioned hootches inhabited by the senior enlisted NCO (non-commissioned officer) types, the army lifers. The officers had their own private Mess Hall, Officer's Club, private hootches, and even their own basketball court. I had no idea how many officers were on the base. They were so invisible that they were not important to any of us.

At the end of the street was a large barn that served as the "operations center" for the 101st Airborne Division. Each function had carved out a section of the giant concrete floor separated by five-foot-high plywood walls marking out their territory. It resembled a present-day cube farm without the cubes but littered with gray steel desks. There were sections for Morning Reports, Special Services, Personnel, and Finance. It was a beehive of activity each day as helicopters flew in from other bases delivering important documents or military personnel seeking to straighten out their records or going home and trying to be awarded their medals and ribbons.

Across from the barn was an amphitheater dug out of the sand consisting of a stage and rows of plank seats where entertainers helped us forget where we were. Most of the bands and singers were Korean or Philippino and pretty good imitators of the American bands we followed back home. Seldom did an American group get this far north but when they did, word spread like wildfire that round-eyed women were in the camp. When the bands weren't in camp, a couple of white bedsheets were hung over the stage forming a movie screen so we could watch reruns from a meagre library of B-level films.

Camp Campbell occupied a section of the perimeter of the camp that we patrolled. Facing out overlooking lush rice paddies, the perimeter was dotted with concrete, fortified bunkers placed one hundred yards apart. Concertina wire was strung in front of the bunkers with fifty-five-gallon drums filled with phosphorescent chemicals that could light up the sky in the event of attack. A Vietnamese cemetery bumped up against the perimeter at one point displaying a variety of headstones and markers for the citizens of Phu Bai Village. At least the army had enough humanity to leave undisturbed the remains of local citizens and relatives. The gesture was one of only a few actions that showed respect for the culture of the local inhabitants.

This was my new neighborhood. It didn't compare with Mount

Greenwood and the block where I was formed and raised. Mount Greenwood today is experiencing gentrification as city workers remodel their homes, adding dormers and swimming pools, even paving streets and alleys and constructing curbs and sewers. Camp Campbell is a distant memory. I think about it once in a while but I don't miss anything about it. I've heard from international travelers who visited the area, that it is now a sandy dune bordered by rice paddies and the lonely Route 1 that ferries travelers to and from the contemporary, attractive Phu Bai International Airport.

Thanks for the memories ...
~BOB HOPE

CHAPTER 18

The Bob Hope Show

The Bob Hope Show, Camp Eagle, Vietnam, December 24, 1971.

One major bright spot during my tour of duty was the arrival of Bob Hope and his band of entertainers. The long Vietnamese monsoon season took a break on December 24, 1971, with the arrival of Hope. We had heard that he was in-country performing and that he was coming our way, but we had no idea of the date. Twenty-four hours in advance of the show, we were notified and given a day off to attend it or just hang around the compound. I jumped at the chance to do something new, so I boarded a two-and-a-half-ton army limo for the trip to Camp Eagle, another base camp of the 101st Airborne about ten miles from our camp. We were treated to a gourmet lunch of C-rations and water that all the guys laughed about. I think our silliness was emblematic of our excitement that war was being interrupted for a few hours and we didn't have to think about it. The sun came out and began to bake us with ninety-degree heat but nobody minded, nobody complained.

The show was at the Eagle Bowl, an amphitheater carved out of a hillside that sat a few thousand guys all wearing the same olive-drab fatigues with the screaming eagle on our arm. We packed ourselves in and waited for Hope and his entourage to appear. It was strangely quiet this day, no big guns thundering, no activity, only the continuous runs of Hueys and Cobras keeping the area outside the base safe from intruders. One solitary, prop-driven cargo plane circled the entire time. We figured it was Hope's plane not wanting to be a target on the ground that could endanger all of us.

The show was OK but not funny. Hope's humor was World War II vintage shtick. His biggest laugh was when he quipped about drugs and marijuana, and his biggest cheer was when he mentioned Phi Bai, the hamlet these huge army bases encircled. It was wonderful seeing gorgeous, round-eyed women again, but I felt like a lion being tantalized with a raw steak. The show ended with all of us singing

"Silent Night," an event I've not forgotten as the years have piled up. Bob Hope has been my hero. He didn't forget us in our unpopular, immoral war. He showed up and loved us! I still carry a fondness for Hope and his company for giving up their holiday celebrations to travel halfway around the world to entertain a bunch of home-sick grunts.

CHAPTER 19

Returning Home

This was the final letter I wrote shortly before returning home.

14 January 1972

Dear Dad:

I'm sitting in the Seattle-Tacoma Airport waiting for my ride home. I'll be seeing you and mom in a few hours but I wanted to tell you of my flight out of Vietnam while it was still fresh in my mind. I left Phu Bai International two days ago after turning [in] my gear and saying good-bye to my buddies. After signing some papers, I was transported by the Army limo, the 2-1/2 ton open bed truck, to the Phu Bai International Airport. There was no plane waiting for us and everyone began to complain and curse the army for screwing us one more time. Eventually, a Chinook helicopter landed and I scrambled aboard. The heat in this aircraft was like a furnace but it felt like the breath of freedom to me. I prayed the entire half hour flight to Danang that we wouldn't get shot down since the Chinook is such a large slow moving target. It took another day of sitting around Danang before we were searched like we were criminals looking for drugs, contraband and Army souvenirs. What a reward for serving your country!

Finally departure day arrived and we boarded onto a silver bird to fly us home. I was so happy to leave this God-forsaken country. My friend Cliff was flying with me. We had both received round trip tickets and were enjoying our departure immensely more than our arrival. As the plane thundered down the runway, I could feel my body begin to shed Vietnam like dirty clothes. But it wasn't until we turned out over the South China Sea and saw Vietnam falling behind us that I could breathe and feel safe. I was going home. At last!

Your son,
Dick

Vietnam was different from World War II in that one day you were sweltering in jungle heat slogging through brown river water, and the next day you stepped off a 707 back into "the world" as we referred to the United States. There was no one to welcome us home. No parades for the heroes' safe return. I think that society wanted to avoid us, ashamed of what they had asked us to do, and appalled at what had happened to many of us.

In many traditional societies, returning soldiers had to undergo a time of purification before being accepted back into society. The Navajo people had a ceremony called 'Anaa 'jf, or the Enemy Way. This process was used for a variety of sicknesses that came from experiences like participation in war. During the first century, Christians who had fought as soldiers had to go through a rehabilitation process that often lasted as long as a year. Christianity taught then that participation in war injured the souls of those who fought.

There was no decompression programs for us who returned from Vietnam—no parades, no welcome home ceremonies, no attempts to acclimate citizen–soldiers into mainstream society. We were in Vietnam one day and then back on the block the next. We were expected to get on with our lives and resume or start our careers and reestablish our relationships that had been strained and stretched through a year of absence. Our fathers had returned from World War II in Europe and the Pacific on troop ships or in cargo planes that gave them time to process what they had endured together with other soldiers. They came home as units, with the men they had served with thus providing therapy for each other with their presence and understanding. In Iraq and Afghanistan, units trained together, went to war together, and returned home together at the end of their deployment. The cohesiveness that they created and nurtured was available for them when they returned.

Vietnam veterans didn't benefit from the homecomings that present-day soldiers experience on a routine basis. I rode the big silver bird to Vietnam with one or two guys I had trained alongside. Once we arrived in-country, we were sorted according to the army's needs and sent to different units ranging from the 5th Mechanized Division and the 101st Airborne in the North to the Americal Division in the Central Highlands to the numerous other bases throughout South Vietnam. We came home when we finished our yearlong tour of duty. We were herded onto passenger jets with other soldiers we didn't know and sent to Fort Lewis, Washington, before we were set free.

The army didn't know what to do with us. There was no final physical exam or psychological assessment to determine our fitness for rejoining society as civilians. I do, however, recall a debriefing by an army officer, a captain who regaled us about how our military experience would stay in our blood for the rest of our lives. He was right, and it would reappear later in our lives when we didn't expect it. I heard about the VA educational benefits I would receive, an explanation I listened to attentively. I intended to enroll in graduate school and pursue an MBA with a concentration in Hospital Administration. The officer encouraged us to remain in the army for an additional thirty days and report to our next duty station. For me, that would have been Fort Hood, Texas. I emphatically refused the generous offer with full knowledge that I would be forfeiting a certain number of months of educational assistance. I was leaving the army that day and no counteroffers were acceptable. This was my ETS day, my Estimated Time of Separation.

I flew to Chicago early the next morning and was greeted at O'Hare Airport by my mom and dad and my good friend John. My dad gave me a huge bear hug, the first I had received since I was a kid. Everyone was emotionally overwhelmed, including me. Although still in uniform, I was no longer on active duty in the US Army. But after my arrival back on the block, I went about becoming a civilian once again without any guidance or mentoring. I had no idea what to expect from the life I had left eighteen months before headed for the unknown in the US Army.

The military knows all about body count,
but neither understands nor acknowledges "soul count."

~ROBERT EMMET MEAGHER,
Killing from the Inside Out

CHAPTER 20

A Wounded Soul

The first meeting of the Class of 2010 of Leadership Greater McHenry County was a self-directed experience the class chose focusing on the arts and the people and places involved in a vast array of artistic endeavors. Convened at the Lakeside Legacy Arts Park in Crystal Lake, Illinois, the morning session of the monthly meetings involved tours of the art studios that were carved out of the venerable landmark also known as the Dole Mansion.

A serpentine line wound its way through the myriad studios where artisans sculpted and applied oil to canvas to interpret the world through their unique lenses. I followed like a lemming into the studio of Jeanine Hill-Soldner, a portrait artist located on the lower level. Suddenly I encountered a wall of portraits of military veterans. My knees weakened as I felt as though I were treading on holy ground. I could sense a story behind each likeness clothed in jungle fatigues, business attire, flight suits, and blue jeans. My eyes wandered from portrait to portrait all the while feeling a sense of belonging, of camaraderie with the faces hanging on the walls.

As I approached the artist, I found that I was at a loss for words. I was as nervous as a groom awaiting his bride, gasping for air, feeling something otherworldly going on around me. After gaping at the array of artwork on display, I finally blurted out a feeble question in a trembling voice, "are you looking for veterans to sit for a portrait?'

Her response was immediate and without the slightest hesitation. "I would love to paint your portrait."

I was stunned at her answer. How did she know who or what I was? Was "Veteran" tattooed on my forehead? Did she and I have some psychic connection or was it a lucky guess? I took her card and promised to call her and set up an appointment.

Within a week, I had scheduled a sitting with Jeanine in her sanctuary of military art. After some initial banter, Jeanine went to work preparing herself and the tools of her trade. I watched with rapt attention as she carefully assembled and positioned the brushes, oils, and canvas surrounding me as I sat in a chair draped in my army dress greens. It was unnerving at first being the focus of the intensity of her work. I wasn't used to the attention, and I wasn't prepared for what was yet to come.

Jeanine began sketching with charcoal, outlining her subject, and as she did she began to relate why she was interested in painting veterans' portraits. Jeanine was the daughter of what we called a "lifer," a career military soldier. A marine, her father had served in World War II, Korea, and Vietnam. He, like many of his contemporaries, never shared his military experiences with his family. He kept his career hidden from his daughter and was frequently on a deployment halfway around the world. After his death, Jeanine attempted to get to know her father through the other military veterans and active-duty personnel she met.

Me posing with my portrait.

The Portraits of American Veterans Project comprises oil paintings of twenty-two soldiers, sailors, marines, and airmen who served in the military from World War II to Afghanistan. She didn't recruit her subjects; they seemed to find her.

Spending two to three hours putting oil on a canvas gave Jeanine the exposure to military life she had never received from her dad. She learned how to ask sensitive questions and to gain access to a storehouse of information and deeply held feelings many family members never take the time to plumb. I found this to be the same experience with my family. It was interesting to me that my family never asked me questions or probed my feelings about my war service. Maybe they felt guilty for not writing to me more often or were afraid to find out what I might tell them. Perhaps they didn't know how to ask the right questions, or maybe they were just glad I was home. My dad never talked with me about my military career, and I was disappointed it was something we never shared since he spent four years in the South Pacific in World War II.

As my sitting began, I found myself telling the artist about my own seventeen-month career of being drafted into the army, molded as a soldier, and then sent to Vietnam. As I dug further into my background,

I began to remember details that had been locked away for forty years. The conversation continued with Jeanine often turning away from the canvas to question me and follow up on issues of particular interest to her, issues that delved into feelings of the guilt of surviving and returning unharmed, learning to kill, and wondering how I would function in a combat unit when gunfire broke out all around me.

I began to sense that I was approaching a precipice, where I was leaning over a cliff, looking down into a chasm of darkness, down a road I feared to tread. Feelings welled up that I had never confronted before and were now dead ahead in front of my eyes. Why did I participate in the Vietnam War? Why didn't I see it as the immoral war that it was? How could I possibly explain away the Fifth Commandment, "Thou Shalt Not Kill"? Suddenly I was uncorking feelings of anger, guilt, and self-loathing that were spawned many years ago even before my induction into the military. As I look back on this journey, I realized that it was at this point in my life, in this art studio, that I began to explore feelings that I have subsequently learned to label as "moral injury."

Another way I'm dealing with my moral injury is through the help of other veterans. The veterans writing workshop, Voices of Veterans, provides me a welcome respite, a place of acceptance and welcome. I have found comfort just being in the presence of other war veterans at these meetings. They understand the language and the military jargon that brings a knowing smile and recognition of a former comrade in arms. In my writer's group, we have written about how we were affected by the deaths and traumatic injuries of fellow soldiers, guys who were close friends, who went through some of the most difficult times of war together. We also wrote about other intensely held times of our lives like the deaths of our fathers and other losses. These sessions have knitted us together like few other opportunities. We have become in a sense "wounded healers" as Henri Nouwen, the prolific writer of books on spirituality, describes. Wounded healers understand the pain because we feel it. We can help heal each other because we carry the scars of battle deep within our souls.

Poetry has been a refuge and source of transformation for me to plumb the feelings that have plagued me these past few years. I wrote about Vietnam and found it was helpful in resurrecting emotion that I hadn't dealt with or hadn't known existed. Poetry puts form on these emotions, expressing them with action-packed words and powerful phrases that are often not possible verbally. It forces me to package complex feelings into words that can be juxtaposed with others to express what conversation cannot.

Jeanine had skillfully probed the ministries that I have explored over the past few years and zoomed in on healing prayer and the laying on of hands. This deeply spiritual practice is something that I have discovered as a gift I possess and is something that is to be shared with and for others. I discovered this spiritual gift in 1998 when, at a healing service at an Episcopal Church, I prayed for the healing of a young man who lived in San Francisco, the son of a colleague from work who had brain cancer. The very day that I received the laying on of hands on his behalf, the cancer began to recede and eventually left him cancer-free. Although it took me ten years to find an outlet for this gift, I eventually founded a healing prayer ministry in my own church. It was this very same healing group that I founded that would be the source of consolation and forgiveness that I needed in my own inner healing.

CHAPTER 21

Soul Repair

Rita Nakashima Brock writes eloquently in her book *Soul Repair* about the case of Dweylon who served in the army in Iraq. Dweylon never fired a weapon, but he felt as morally guilty of killing innocent people as those who did:

> "I don't want to equate what I did to those who had to kill people. I know I cannot imagine having to do that, to stare down your gun at someone, squeeze the trigger, and see them dead—to have the courage to do that and then to adjust to this when you come home. When I think about my own role, it messes with me, because I didn't squeeze a trigger, but I did the same thing."[1]

---

1   Rita Nakashima Brock, *Soul Repair, Recovering from Moral Injury after War* (Boston: Beacon Hill, 2012), 58.

Dweylon was not proud to wear the uniform, carry a rifle, or be part of what was done in Iraq. He loved his country but felt no one should be proud of an unnecessary war.

I struggled constantly with the reality of being thrust into a combat role and being forced to engage the enemy during a firefight. I worried about not protecting my buddies by trying not to kill, by aiming away from the enemy even if I couldn't see them. I worried about my own safety if I didn't shoot to kill. These thoughts tormented me, and I hadn't even arrived in Vietnam at that point.

As the war dragged on, I learned that many grunts went out on patrol and refused to fight and flush out the NVA or Vietcong. Many refused to leave base camp and defied their superior officers, who feared getting fragged by the soldiers under their command.

Maybe I would have spent eleven months humping the bush and never encountering enemy gunfire. I may have never had to discharge my weapon, obey a command to kill innocent civilians, nor sit in an ambush waiting, hoping no one would enter the killing zone. But living with this unknown terror was a daily and constant preoccupation. I didn't worry about being killed; I worried about killing. I worried that my soul would suffer for eternity for taking another human life. I also worried a lot about what combat would do to me, to the person I was, to my essence, my very soul.

Would I become a battle-hardened killer? While I looked with disdain at the Vietnamese people, would I be able to kill innocent civilians as they did at My Lai? I'm sure that my moral upbringing would have caused me to speak out, to let my superiors know that I was being asked to do something I knew was wrong. But how would that have been received? Did my commanding officers have the time or the inclination to work through my ethical dilemmas when they had their orders? After all, they had a war to fight.

I do believe that if I had engaged in combat, I would be living with terrible guilt today and much graver self-loathing than what I'm experiencing now. I've thought about the war every day for over forty years. How could I live with causing the death of other human beings? I'd be a basket case spending hours on the psychiatric couch. Maybe the horror of combat would have made me a pacifist committed to finding forgiveness and peace for the wrongs I had done. It's only conjecture at this point. I'll never know except in my memoir writing and poetry. And that may be the answer, a way through this pain and regret. I pray that it is.

It was fate that I found Rita Brock and her work with veterans seeking the repair of their souls. I have found that I'm far from being alone and, in fact, may be ahead of a lot of my comrades who haven't dealt with the war and their role in it. I'm anxious to do more work on this and find a way to receive forgiveness and peace for my troubled soul.

CHAPTER 22

Gooks

The moral wrongs and indiscretions that I and my fellow soldiers committed extended beyond the battlefield. I didn't see the Vietnamese people as human beings. I was taught through army training that they were "gooks." Gook was a derogatory term used by the US military during wartime toward East and Southeast Asians, especially Koreans and Vietnamese. The small souvenir shop just inside the perimeter of our camp that was operated by locals was referred to as the "gook shop." They were also referred to as "dinks," an extremely disparaging and contemptuous slang word directed at people from the region of Southeast Asia and Vietnam.

I despised the Vietnamese women who worked in our camp doing the tasks we wouldn't do—like hauling away the garbage and cleaning latrines. They wore black-silk clothing we called pajamas that were actually known as "ao dai" and conical straw hats, known as "non la," to shield their faces from the sun. Thongs were the dress of the day for their feet, which forced them to have a shuffling style of gait, the walk of slaves or servants. These beautiful, traditional articles of clothing were looked down upon rather than revered, identifying them not as partners or allies but rather as inferior servants. I hated them for all of that. I probably felt as I did because I didn't want to be in their country, so I demeaned their language, their customs, and their traditional dress.

I didn't trust the Vietnamese that I saw. I had seen the news reports of US soldiers killed by Vietnamese children who carried and detonated hand grenades among groups of soldiers. I was afraid they would steal from us if we didn't secure our possessions. In fact, one day I was assigned to guard the garbage truck as it picked up trash around our base camp. One of our guys noticed that one of the Vietnamese men had buried a steel pot under a pile of garbage on the truck. He screamed and threatened the offender so loudly that I could read the hatred in the eyes of the lowly thief. Chances are that the army wouldn't have missed the pot, but it was one man's attempt to control and assert his superiority over people he hated.

I learned to call the older men "*papa-sanh*" and the women "*mama-sanh*," or "*baby-sanh*" to the young women. The army has a penchant for assigning derogatory titles to people that are considered enemies or different. "*Mama-sanh*" referred to a woman in Southeast Asia—chiefly in Japan—who was in charge of a geisha house or nightclub. "*Papa-sanh*" was also a derogatory term referring to an elderly man who was a pimp. These obviously were not the terms of endearment that I thought they were. But it was the army way of labeling people to be thought of as subhuman, mere objects, so that when GIs were ordered to set fire to the hootches in villages and hamlets, they wouldn't feel like they were killing other human beings; they were only killing "gooks."

Vietnamese women were subjugated into other despicable roles that became commonly accepted on our base camp. Local women operated the Latin Quarter Steam and Massage, a massage parlor referred to in army parlance as the "steam and cream." Massages were advertised, but sexual favors were the real reason soldiers frequented this establishment. This business must have infuriated the Vietcong because one night our camp received mortar fire targeted specifically at the massage parlor, leveling it to the ground.

The hootch I inhabited with five other guys was used as a brothel one evening before we returned from our work. As I approached our hootch, I noticed a line of guys waiting outside. The soldier who served as the pimp approached me, offering me complimentary services for the trouble of using my home for the comfort services of his customers. In short, the Vietnamese were viewed as less than human, and these immoral acts were viewed as a small price for them to pay for the defense of their country.

CHAPTER 23

Soul Fragmentation

The shamans have a term for it, *fragmentation* of the soul. It occurs in one's past from a trauma or a series of events that bring great sadness or loss. In my case, the traumas that I can recount were the loss of my first love, the death of my dad, a major job loss, and serving in the army in Vietnam. I have dealt with the first three well. For example, I have found a new, deeper love life as opposed to the infatuation that claimed my heart in my early twenties.

Karen entered my life on the eighth floor of Marshall Field & Company in downtown Chicago. I had been back from Nam for a few months when I decided I needed a job to tide me over until I began grad school in September of 1972. A friend offered me a job as a furniture salesman at the most prestigious department store on State Street. After a few weeks of scouting the territory where beautiful young women worked as interior designers and sales associates, a gorgeous creature walked into my life in the middle of the upholstered furniture, antiques, and dining-room suites. I knew immediately that I wanted to get to know her. Something mystical happened that I had never experienced before.

We lunched often and confided in each other about our love lives. One of our conversations occurred on the twelfth floor, the employee cafeteria, when I talked about my reluctance to talk about my Vietnam experience since the country was still embroiled in the war and returning soldiers were called baby killers and drug addicts. Karen prophesied that in the future, my military service would be valued and celebrated as a feeling of patriotism would return to our country. Well, she nailed that one and endeared me to her so much so that I forgot about all others, and we have been together ever since. Now forty-six years later, I realize that the fragmentation I had experienced was healed in that encounter on State Street.

The death of my dad was sudden. A massive coronary jolted him from my life at a time when he and I were spending time together on the golf course and at his retirement home in Southwest Michigan. I got to know him as a man, and he saw his son grow up, succeed in business, and begin a family. At first, the suddenness of his death was overwhelming since he was vigorous and active. I felt heartache with a literal pain in my chest for a month after his dying. Time has healed this wound as the anniversaries of his death have glided past and I have learned to treasure the happy memories of his presence in my life.

I was dealt a devastating blow when I was fired from a fantastic job as CEO of a hospital in Asheville, North Carolina. Even though I saw it as the culmination of my career, I found that forces were plotting behind the scenes to discredit me and reverse many of the successes I had achieved. I was called a Yankee every day for the three years I spent on the job. What I wasn't prepared for was the passive/aggressive resentment from my senior staff who had not been considered for the position when the board did a CEO search and instead chose someone from the outside to be the new leader.

It was a lethal blow at first, but I rebounded by starting a business together with my wife, Karen. We bought a recruitment franchise from Management Recruiters International and moved back to Chicago, back to our roots, back to family and friends. While the business was not successful, the move gave us a chance to reinvent ourselves and take up career paths in companion directions. I entered the senior living industry and Karen rejoined the banking industry. We put the dark days of North Carolina behind us and have never looked back.

But the fragmentation of my soul that occurred in my military career has returned to haunt me and raise deep, ethical concerns about my role in the Vietnam War. It was different from other issues that brought grief and sorrow but immediately dissipated like dew on the morning grass. This role revisited my consciousness forty years after I was discharged from the army. It has ignited feelings of guilt and shame, feelings I didn't experience over all those years when I was pursuing my career aspirations and raising a family.

The shaman would offer that these fragments of the soul that were lost can be recovered. They are pieces of the soul lost in time, still alive and capable of being reintegrated with the rest of the soul. I know very little about this process, but it is interesting that it was brought to my attention and that the process of *soul retrieval* is being mentioned as a legitimate therapy for veterans from the Vietnam War. Ray Leonardi writes in his meditation on moral injury:

"Moral Injury is a wound to the soul, caused by participation in events that violate one's most deeply held sense of right and wrong. The perpetrator realizes how wrong it was. The irony is that the disorder is actually an appropriate normal response to an overwhelmingly abnormal situation."[1]

Different types of one-to-one therapy are not effective in dealing with moral injury. Rohr[2] claims that practices like *centering prayer* are uniquely designed to heal these types of wounds. *Centering prayer* bypasses the mind with the horrific memories and trauma and invites participants to detach from their stories and let go into the surrounding silence. There they can encounter God or the divine through speaking with the heart. Establishing this direct sense of communication allows the moral injury or shame to release, and then the person can begin to forgive him- or herself.

1   Ray Leonardi, in a Meditation from, "Healing Our Social Wounds," the Center for Action and Contemplation, September 26, 2017.

2   Richard Rohr, "Healing Our Social Wounds," the Center for Action and Contemplation, September 26, 2017.

"They can begin to forgive themselves and feel like they just might be lovable."

~RAY LEONARDI

CHAPTER 24

Forgiveness

That may be what I'm searching for, forgiveness. That may be at the heart of my quest for peace and the healing of a soul fractured and forced to do things that were antithetical to its purpose. Forgiveness seemed to be at the heart of the problem for me when I sought healing from my Order of St. Luke (OSL) healing team. The Order of St. Luke is an interdenominational healing ministry that promotes physical, spiritual, and emotional healing through prayer and the laying on of hands.

During one of our biweekly meetings, I expressed a need to be healed from the memories of war. I couldn't describe it very well at the time; in fact, I was quite emotionally crippled at the time and was at a loss for words. I didn't know where to turn, and then God appeared. God appeared in the circle of people who laid hands on me and prayed for me. They prayed for God to heal my memories. But the words that brought the most comfort, the most relief, the real sense of healing came from Bill Kruse, our chaplain. Bill laid his hands on me and said, "Dick, you no longer have to worry about these memories that trouble you. You are forgiven for the things you did and the things you did not do." Right then I felt a wave of relief wash over me. The veil of shame and guilt lifted, and I felt the forgiveness experienced in a confessional box.

I didn't think it was possible to heal myself. Why? I was in the healing ministry as a healer, but I had difficulty finding my own forgiveness. This instance was just that—a point in time. The sense of guilt and need for forgiveness would reoccur many times in the future, but the intervals between these outbreaks would become longer.

Another occasion comes to mind when the guilt and shame returned. I arrived at work and related my struggle with the anxiety that accompanies moral injury to the chaplain at our senior living community. His words hit home. He told me that God had forgiven me, but I hadn't learned to forgive myself. He was right. I had been carrying the guilt around with me like a red badge of courage refusing to give it up, wearing it openly in spite of the pain.

A South Vietnamese orphan near a barbed-wire fence.

In a book of poetry I published entitled, *Healing Memories*, I addressed the emotions that led me through eleven months of Vietnam, emotions of guilt and forgiveness and becoming a man nine thousand miles from home.

The poem, "Forgiveness," captured the need that I felt forty years later. The poem is printed adjacent to a photograph of a South Vietnamese orphan standing behind a barbed-wire fence, emblematic of the life that children endured during the war.

Forgiveness

Memories haunt the hidden mind
Fed by the cadence of time,
Reluctant warriors feel the stench
Ignited in a youthful soul.

Nausea erupts in the knowledge
Triggered by the explosive siege,
The bond of brothers shakes with images
Born of brokenness and loss.

Discontent devours the mindful peace
Left in the wake of immoral destruction,
Scores of memories recreate the sentence
Seared into the brain by guilt and shame.

Emotions belch up from a distant past
Suppressed by years of conscious neglect,
Peace reigns again dispensed from loving hands
Blessed with the sign of forgiveness.[1]

---

1   Dick Hattan, *Healing Memories* (Woodstock: Xlibris, 2010).

So, if it's forgiveness that is the problem for me, how do I deal with it? It seems to me that the path to wholeness is to find forgiveness from the people who were so deeply hurt by the crime. I've heard of veterans who have returned to Vietnam for their own healing and have found the Vietnamese to be welcoming to the interlopers who tore up their country and helped fight their civil war. The serendipitous reunions provided balm for both sides, all sides, of the war, but something more needs to be done.

The United States didn't have a Marshall Plan as it did after World War II where Germany was rebuilt by US aid. It didn't open its coffers in Southeast Asia to invest in the fragile economy of Vietnam; the victorious North Vietnam and China prohibited that. It did help a limited number of refugees as they attempted to escape the onslaught of the North Vietnamese Army. But many left the shores of their native land in small, overcrowded fishing boats and were drowned in the stormy waters of the South China Sea. But, it wasn't enough. The United States wanted to forget the war and move on. The filming of combat and burning of thatched hootches was exhausting the American public.

The absence of a rebuilding program and economic development provided little opportunity for US veterans to stretch out a hand of support amid the sorrow. I don't feel an urgency to return to Vietnam. Participating in a rebuilding program or some other acts of reparation would be another iteration of the colonial imperialism that has beset this land since the French occupation. Corporate America has begun to create jobs and manufacture goods in Vietnam for competition around the world. My involvement would be meaningless.

What we need is a time of forgiveness. We don't need a parade or some national recognition day for Vietnam veterans. It's too late for that, and we need more than another outpouring of patriotic fervor; that might only serve to further confuse or conflict many of us who aren't proud of our military experience. I'm thinking of a national gathering at the Wall in Washington, DC, and at other Vietnam memorials throughout the country. This would be a National Day of Forgiveness with speeches, prayers, songs, and silence where veterans could find expression for the sorrow they have felt and the regret in their souls about being part of the United States war machine in Vietnam. We need to find a venue to tell our stories to each other, to comfort one another and forgive each other. This public expression could provide the balm and forgiveness to those suffering from moral injury and might knit together our fractured souls.

CHAPTER 25

Questions, Questions

Why is there a pecking order in the military? Why are the combat vets the most esteemed? Why are the grunts, the infantry guys, treated as heroes? The killers, the guys squeezing the trigger, are the most admired. Why do soldiers re-up for Iraq and Afghanistan? Why do they want to go back and finish what was started? Why leave their families to face death, to create war, to have a job of taking other lives?

Why do I get so conflicted about all this? Why don't I become a serious pacifist and never wear my veteran's cap, disavow my military service. Instead, I want the recognition for serving but have conflict in my head for being part of a killing machine that took so many lives.

I have found myself thinking or wishing I should have been in combat so I'd have that experience. But would it have been enough? Would I have wanted more? More firefights, more people killed, more war stories to tell?

I'd never be satisfied with what I'd done, or I'd have to live with the aftermath, the visuals, the memories of being a combat veteran—the night sweats, the nightmares, the anger, the guilt. The swagger that many combat veterans exhibit is false pride. It wouldn't have worked with me. The guilt I currently feel would be magnified. Trying to find a lasting sense of forgiveness would be a lifelong quest. I've never experienced despair because I am and always have been such a positive person and feel so loved, yet this would have been a challenge for me. I think about Vietnam every day as it is. I can't imagine how thoughts of killing and destruction would have further occupied my mind and haunted my soul.

CHAPTER 26

No, Thanks!

"Thank you for your service."

I'm tired of hearing it. It's shallow and meaningless. I don't know what to say anymore. The words ring hollow without emotion like being repeated from a taped message from a robo call. Nobody cared that I spent eleven months of my young-adult life in Southeast Asia, part of America's war machine back in 1971. I hid away any reminders of Vietnam back in the recesses of my mind and charged ahead with a family and a career that took me to four different states. Nothing was ever said about my military service. I couldn't understand the silence. Were people afraid of what I had done? Were they afraid to ask for fear they'd awaken a raging psychopath who'd go ballistic or reach out to strangle them to death? Now looking back, I feel they didn't understand what I had to do and probably didn't want to know.

With the advent of the wars in the Middle East, patriotism has returned and now swells in the hearts of the twenty-thousand-plus Chicago Blackhawks fans each night on the ice of the United Center. Tears come to the eyes of baby boomers whose kids have enlisted in the army or marines. At parades and on the street of my little town, people notice my "Vietnam Veteran" cap and feel compelled to thank me for my service. I'm beginning to resent the words. It reminds me of what we say to each other at wakes and funerals: "I'm sorry for your loss."

The words are hollow, devoid of emotion, and don't convey the sincere feelings of sorrow and grief we often feel. It's the same phrase repeated without impact, without emotion. But I also feel that I don't want to be reminded of what I was part of forty years ago. If I could do it differently, I would today. These well-wishers can't give me back what I lost; they can't let me relive that time in my life that seems now to have been wasted.

Only other Vietnam veterans seem to know and understand. We always want to ask each other questions like: When were you over there? Where did you serve? Who were you with? They seemed to open the door and let down one's guard. The most acceptable phrase that I've heard is, "Welcome home." It says it all. It acknowledges what we went through and says something from one veteran to another that our country didn't say to us.

CHAPTER 27

Writing Poetry to Heal

I began to write poetry as an outgrowth of journaling that I started twenty-five years ago to relieve the stress from my career. While journal writing was helpful as an emotional release, I discovered that writing poetry went much deeper. The juxtaposition of words and phrases packed the power, guilt, and sadness that journaling did not. The outward expression that I discovered helped me to explore thoughts and feelings I thought were dangerous, unpatriotic, and shameful. Fashioning words into poetic form brought relief and unexplored emotions that I would never have consciously admitted. My poem, "Growing up in Vietnam," told my story of the fear and death that surrounded me as I experienced the pains of becoming an adult.

Growing Up in Vietnam

Sweat-drenched days collided with an endless stream of
Boring darkness on the bunkered perimeter,
"Papa Sanhs" skipped across green-tipped rice paddies,
While water buffalo grazed unhunted amid the war's scream
　　of death.

Though they never came, I waited for their stealth-like crawl,
Terror lit my heart as the tapes replayed
My life before this jungle,
Why was I here, while others heard a different call?

The ancient tombs spoke of past elegance,
As faded paint on Hue's palace displayed forgotten hope.
Brown water and rocks pounded clothes into anger,
But the war machine lurched forward without vision.

Safe in my metal shell, I was spared the blood,
Even birds carrying the dead from battle flew unhindered,
But I crashed into its path as I heard the news about
His legs that lost to a claymore's advance.

Eleven months ended my sentence but not without the pain
Of growing up in Vietnam, finally a man,
Was it worth the fear of killing amid homesick starvation?
The questions never cease while my mind never rests.[1]

Poetry provided an outlet and ultimately a source of healing from
the memories and guilt that besieged me after the war was over for me.
I used some of my black-and-white photographs of me and the area

---

1　　Hattan, 27.

around me to help tap into the emotions that I was going through and recapture what life was like for me back then. The poem, "Guilt," was printed next to a pensive image of me in my jungle fatigues seated at a makeshift desk in my hootch. I remember sitting there like it was yesterday writing letters to my friends and family trying to create a semblance of happiness in the middle of a war zone. The poem is an attempt to address survivor's guilt, anger, and a plea for healing that would consume me for a lifetime.

Guilt

War without battle scars
Sews confusion and guilt
Over leaving comrades in
Jungles of fear and horror.

Engagement in a foreign land
Where hate learns to survive,
Implicit in the war machine
The growth of 40-year-old guilt.

Arriving on the sterile tarmac
To a hero's solitary parade,
A final curtain drops on the
Yearlong sentence of death.

Guilt gallops through the memories
Of Agent Orange and severed limbs,
A peaceful warrior wades through
Reopened wounds of confusing choices.

A search for healing and rest
Becomes a purposeful journey

Back to a youthful age of
Killing fear and faceless hell.[2]

---

2   Hattan, 29.

CHAPTER 28

Parker Palmer and Discovering My Calling

Parker Palmer, in his great little book, *Let Your Life Speak,* writes from his Quaker background about his notion of "call," about the discovery of a person's vocation in life. He writes about twenty-one carefully chosen and artfully woven words given to him to express the quest for vocation:

> "Now I become myself.
> It's taken time, many years and places.
> I have been dissolved and shaken,
> Worn other people's faces ..."[1]

---

1   May Sarton, "Now I Become Myself," in *Let Your Life Speak* by Parker Palmer (San Francisco: Jossey Bass, 2000), 9.

He advises to look back over one's lifetime to see the common threads that are woven throughout it. Looking back over his own career and the varied positions he occupied, he found a common thread in teaching. He was called by God to be a teacher, and it manifested itself in the variety of positions and professions he occupied.

In my life, I made the decision to seek out a career in health-care management, a decision that came to me while on guard duty protecting the perimeter of our base camp in Vietnam. While peering through the concertina wire and observing life in the rice paddies surrounding my view, I became aware of what I wanted my next career path to be. It occurred to me that I could pursue my ambition of leading a successful business career and satisfy the altruism that I have always felt was an important aspect of life. I followed through on that revelation and have enjoyed a successful career as a health-care executive at a comfortable distance from the bedside where the actual healing takes place through the skillful hands of doctors and nurses. As my career advanced, I decided to explore career options in the senior living industry, inching closer to the patients and the family surrounding them. In looking at these and other threads in my life, I discovered that my calling was to be a healer.

I found myself drawn to pastoral care in my church and ultimately back to the seminary where I would take up theological education. A core piece of the Master of Divinity curriculum is the Clinical Pastoral Education experience in a hospital setting where a student learns pastoral care at the bedside through hands-on practice, trial and error, where some of the most transformational events take place. I found that I came alive as a chaplain. Among other things, I was at the bedsides of dying people and prayed with people who were terminally ill. These were phenomenal experiences that served to solidify my sense that healing was the common thread that held my past careers together.

So, as I contemplated my role as a soldier in the Vietnam War, I realized that *I* needed healing; I couldn't heal myself. I needed to receive healing and forgiveness from God but also from other people in my life.

CHAPTER 29

The Order of St. Luke and My Focus on Healing

Healing became a focus for me. It really has been a thread that has connected my various jobs and avocations all my life. It wasn't so much physical healing that attracted me, although that was part of it, but I was drawn to the spiritual and emotional wholeness that was part of it, often called "inner healing." When I met Father Bill Kruse at the parish picnic on a gorgeous fall day, I learned for the first time about the Order of St. Luke, a healing ministry grounded in the ethos of the Episcopal Church. Bill, a retired Episcopal priest, had organized a chapter of the Order at a neighboring church. Fate was involved in this meeting for both of us. Bill didn't want to retire completely from the healing ministry after he left his last parish as an associate rector. He saw in me a potential partner, a person with the energy and enthusiasm to rekindle the fire to serve people who needed healing.

The Holy Spirit was at work that day, I have no doubt in my mind. For me, Bill was the spiritual guide I needed to help chart a course and provide the sage advice that a new venture needed to succeed. We assembled a group of eight to ten people who expressed some interest in this ministry and began meeting twice a month to educate ourselves about healing prayer and to learn how to do it by practicing on each other.

Praying aloud was uncomfortable for me. Catholics didn't pray out loud and neither did Episcopalians, so it was a stretching exercise like trying on a new pair of shoes that felt tight and uncomfortable until you walked around in and worn them a bit. But I learned to lay hands on others and ask God to bring them the healing balm they sought. One of the byproducts of healing prayer is the feeling of warmth and energy that is generated during the laying on of hands. There is an exchange of energy that occurs that adherents in this ministry recognize as the action of the Holy Spirit sending divine energy to the person in need through the hands of the minister. This feeling is often accompanied by mental images or words of comfort that are thought to be evidence of God's presence in the healing encounter.

I joined the Order of St. Luke and threw myself into it with enthusiasm. I became the convener of the group—organizing meetings, preparing agendas, and running meetings. Eventually, I became the chaplain of our chapter. I organized a healing mission that brought seventy-five people to our little church to learn about how God heals through ordinary people like us. Our chapter met to study the healing stories of Jesus and learned to pray with others at monthly liturgies in our church. Eventually, I published an article about my experiences in the healing ministry entitled, "Healing Memories of War."[1]

---

1   Dick Hattan, "Healing Memories of War," in *Healing, The Journal of the Order of St Luke* (October, 2013).

Another avenue for healing the memories of war was my involvement in a veterans writing workshop. At the leadership program that I joined in 2010, I met Mary Margaret Maule, a navy wife and mother of two navy veterans. Mary Margaret and I became kindred spirits when we were asked to participate on a nonprofit board that oversaw a multimillion dollar federal grant for the care and treatment of veterans and family members who were experiencing mental health issues because of their military service.

The two of us decided to venture out on our own to develop a program where veterans could tell their stories in a written format through prose and poetry. With the financial assistance of local rotary clubs, we convened a group of veterans on a biweekly basis to write about their military experiences and express their feelings about their military experiences in a safe, nonjudgmental environment.

The group is now in its fifth year with three of the original members still involved. To date, we have welcomed twenty-five veterans into the group who served from World War II to Afghanistan. We recently added a Gold Star mother to our ranks, providing a safe haven and outlet for her as she grapples with the loss of her son.

Writing and meeting with this group has been a great experience for me. Not only have I profited from the experience of putting my feelings on paper, but I have gotten to know a group of people I now call my friends. The companionship and good-natured ribbing has been a part of my life that I don't want to give up. The veterans writing workshop, Voices of Veterans, provides me a welcome respite, a place of acceptance and welcome. I have found comfort just being in the presence of other war veterans at these meetings. They understand the language and the military jargon that bring a knowing smile and recognition of a former comrade in arms.

In my writer's group, we have written about how we were affected by the deaths and traumatic injuries of fellow soldiers, guys who were close friends, people we went through the war together with. We also wrote about other intensely held times of our lives like the deaths of our fathers and other personal losses. These sessions have knitted us together like few other opportunities. We have become, in a sense, "wounded healers" as Henri Nouwen, the prolific writer of books on spirituality, describes and as I talked about before. Wounded healers understand the pain because we feel it. We can help heal each other because we all carry the scars of battle deep within our souls.

Poetry has been a refuge and source of transformation for me to plumb the depths of the feelings that have plagued me these past few years. I wrote about Vietnam and found it was helpful in resurrecting emotions that I hadn't dealt with or hadn't even known existed. Poetry puts form on these emotions, expressing them with action-packed words and powerful phrases that are often not possible verbally. It forces me to package complex feelings into words that can be juxtaposed with others to express what conversation cannot. It is a vehicle that I use to decompress after times of grief and elation that forces me to probe my inner thoughts and get at the heart of what eats at my soul.

CHAPTER 30

*Ken Burns at the Union
League Club of Chicago
PBS on Vietnam*

I attended a luncheon at the Union League Club in Chicago featuring Ken Burns, the prolific producer of documentaries on fascinating subjects such as the Roosevelts, baseball, World War II, and a number of other films. Burns spoke about his newest documentary, *Vietnam,* previewing the epic story of war, protest, and redemption. I had hoped to learn what Burns had taken from this ten-year opus. I hoped that it would open other doors for me as I plumbed my own feelings about the war and my small part in its prosecution. Perhaps the documentary would stir up conversations about how to talk about war, why we are drawn into it, and why we can't settle our differences peacefully. Perhaps it would answer all the questions I had.

In the preview that opened the documentary series on Vietnam, the narrator showed pictures of present-day Saigon, now Ho Chi Minh City, and Hanoi with their gleaming buildings, bustling streets, and prosperous-looking people. The comment of his that struck me was, "You have to look hard to find evidence of the war." I've heard this from friends who visited Vietnam as tourists. They had to search for the war museums and the entrances to the tunnels that the Vietcong had used to infiltrate US military bases and rural hamlets. The large combat bases like Eagle, Campbell, and Evans of the 101st Airborne have been demolished, their stories and secrets quieted amid the shifting sands and rice paddies that populate the countryside along Highway 1.

It's hard to find evidence of the Vietnam War here in the United States as well. The war that fractured a mighty nation is unknown to the majority of citizens of North America. At that preview of *Vietnam* at the Union League Club of Chicago, a packed house of 350 people sat in rapt attention to the well-spoken Ken Burns and Lynne Novick, his collaborator. The crowd, although dominated by silver-haired remnants of the 1960s, contained a mere handful of military veterans who served in the war. A warm welcome received the aging warriors, but when the luncheon dispersed, the veterans in attendance melted into the bustling sidewalks unrecognized, soon to be forgotten in the mainstream of society.

Their wounds, though, are carried deep within their souls and reemerge in dreams, flashbacks, and in other everyday reminders of their youth in a conflict forever seared into their memories. They carry a burden that doesn't ease even with the passage of decades. In fact, the memories have intensified as they revisit the purpose of their lives and the value of what they did in the folly of their youth.

As the camera turned back to Burns in the preview, he spoke about the difficulty of attempting such a monumental opus. With his collaborators and the advice of military historians and veterans, Burns focused on all sides of the war, peering back through the eyes of former North Vietnamese Army soldiers, Vietcong guerillas, soldiers of the Army of the Republic of Vietnam Nationals (ARVN), and the complex audiences in the United States protesting the war and advocating for its success.

The scope of the effort appealed to me intellectually. I had never heard the pain expressed firsthand from the people of North Vietnam nor heard the reactions of former enemy soldiers. But as Burns continued to explain how they decided to film the war story, he said very emphatically, "If you weren't in combat, you're not in the film." I felt a punch to the gut that I hadn't expected to hear. This was my war, my life. Eleven months gouged out of my young life that ended up on the cutting-room floor.

The protestors at Kent State and the 1968 Democratic Convention in Chicago got the exposure and camera time. They went home after the last bars of "Blowing in the Wind" were sung by Peter, Paul, and Mary. They dispersed after the Chicago cops attacked them with billy clubs sending them back to the comfort of their parents' bungalows and suburban trilevels. Guys like me slept in hootches or in concrete bunkers or on jungle foliage wondering whether we'd awaken to a new day.

I was disappointed with Burns for making that comment. It served to further denigrate my presence in the war especially when I have been so conflicted about my role as a soldier. Couldn't Burns have provided some focus on the moral destruction that the war rained on guys like me who struggled with whether to join or flee? Couldn't there have been a theological perspective on the wounding of a person's soul when he or she is asked to so something against his or her moral code? Why didn't Burns bring in the failure of the churches to speak out? As far as I could tell, his group of advisors to the film didn't include a theologian or the head of a large church body. The generals and military historians were in evidence to analyze the prosecution of the war, but no one was present to address the moral consequences of the war. No one spoke about the psychological damage that is now emerging as former soldiers look for purpose in their lives and ask deep, penetrating questions of themselves. They are asking questions whose answers are difficult to accept and are finding a need to resolve the conflict in their souls that won't go away when they are thanked for their service by the unsuspecting, well-meaning public.

I've learned that Vietnam has had a far-reaching impact on my own generation, the baby boomers. My friends who avoided being drafted during the late sixties and early seventies suffered also. They, too continue to question their motivation, their sense of survivor's guilt at staying home while many of us acquiesced to the draft notices we received. This came home to me with shocking suddenness at a spiritual retreat of Episcopal men that I attended a few years ago with an old friend. I found that the other attendees, regardless of whether they served in Vietnam or became teachers or clergy or joined the Peace Corps, all had felt the pain of loss, of uncertainty, and the questioning of moral values amid pressure from peers who served and fathers who flew the flag as World War II veterans.

The war has touched all of us, but some more than others. I have felt the need to apologize, to express regret, and to wish I had chosen another path to military service. It's something I will live with forever and will continue to seek healing to repair.

Perhaps an answer to this dilemma lies in the failure of the all-volunteer army that allows less than 1 percent of the population of the United States to feel the burden of waging war, learning to hate and kill other people. With 99 percent of the population safely pursuing their career dreams, raising families, and going about a peaceful lifestyle, the onus of committing murder in the name of Democracy falls to the select few. Universal conscription was horrendous for those caught up in the stranglehold of an immoral war, but at least it brought about dissent and protest against the bravado and aggressive posturing of a nation that thought it had God on its side. That myth, that God is on the side of the United States, is simply that, a myth. A nation at war is not a nation under God.

Perhaps our nation's veterans are bringing clarity to the great expense, the great moral cost of any war. These revelations by the people who suffered through war should provide clarity to the American Church that it can no longer sit on the sidelines and pretend war is to be condoned. Our nation that sends young people off to war as heroes and heaps praise on them when they return can no longer be innocent of the guilt and shame that participation in war presents to those who wage war, regardless of their job in the war effort.

CONCLUSION

Facing moral injury should not be a solitary task. A great many of our nation's institutions played a role in sending me and thousands of others like me into a war zone to kill and destroy. We didn't totally understand what we would be asked to do and never had the option of saying, "No thanks, I'd rather not" or "I believe war is immoral; it's wrong to kill."

The church that prepared me, that formed my beliefs and instilled the value system that inhabits my body and soul, must not stand idly by and have nothing to say. It has to help restore the souls fragmented by participating in the horrors of war. It has to welcome them home to the spiritual community that allowed them to leave. The church must provide the opportunities for veterans to share their stories and listen without passing judgment. It needs to train those who didn't enter the killing fields to approach veterans without their own agendas and to learn to respect the reluctance veterans have to share their pain. The church can provide the places where forgiveness can be imparted again and again. Once veterans can seek and feel forgiveness from God, then perhaps they can begin the process of forgiving themselves.

I have begun to understand this phenomenon myself but not without hours of soul-searching and helpful conversations. I have sought forgiveness and received it. Now I have to learn to let it go. I have to release myself from being tormented by guilt. I fear that this will be a lifelong effort where I need to find other ways to find peace.

I wrote a sufficient number of poems that I published in a book entitled *Healing Memories*, a collection of thirty poems chronicling events of my life, including a number of poems describing life in Vietnam. A poem that I penned a few years later recounts my irritation with the attempt by the general public to extend a long overdue welcome by use of the phrase, "*thank you for your service.*" This overused phrase is a feeble attempt by many to assuage their own guilt for sending us off to war and making us out to be heroes. I feel my own guilt well up at these moments instead of experiencing the adulation afforded a conqueror's welcome. The public needs to know that they bear a greater responsibility when they allow their government to engage in war and send their young people off to kill in the name of Democracy and all that is good.

As another attempt at forgiveness and reconciliation with the divine, I've considered but rejected returning to Vietnam on a healing mission. I've become aware of veterans who have returned, performing healing rituals led by skilled therapists and engaging the Vietnamese people in acts of forgiveness. This well-intentioned exercise might benefit some, but I look at it as an extension of our imperialistic presence in the world. If I were Vietnamese, I wouldn't trust these gray-bearded warriors whose country continues to attempt to make the world safe by violence. Any attempt at reconciliation would have to be supported by the full weight of the US government, and I think the American people and their elected officials lack the intestinal fortitude to spend any more tax dollars in Vietnam.

This stint in the US Army with the 101st Airborne Division has turned out to be a seminal event in my life. I'm sure it was also a seminal event in the lives of many other young men who did what they were asked, often unwillingly, but were afraid to refuse. Not a day has gone by since January 15, 1972, when I came home and returned to civilian life, that I don't think about the army, Vietnam, and the life interrupted by a letter with the notorious salutation, "Greetings."

There is a story in the book of Genesis where Jacob crossed the Jabbok River to meet his brother Esau.[1] Jacob got into a wrestling match with a man that lasted all night. When the man realized he couldn't overpower Jacob, he struck him on the hip socket, dislocating his hip. Jacob called the place Peniel because he had seen God's face and lived. Jacob left the scrum with God with a limp that he carried around with him for the rest of his life.

I believe that like Jacob, I struggled with God and was left with my own limp, the moral injury to my soul from my military service in Vietnam. As in the biblical story, no one was there to help me. I wrestled alone and was left with a reminder of the encounter. The injury I carry is a reminder of God's forgiveness that drives me toward wholeness and gratitude.

The moral injury doesn't let me forget and has served as motivation to claim my identity as a pastor, a spiritual leader, not just for other veterans but also in other realms of life. This motivation led me to

---

1   Genesis: 32:22-31 (New Revised Standard Version).

reenter the seminary, and over a twenty-year period, achieve a Master of Divinity degree. It moved me to seek ordination as a priest and build thriving ministries with nursing-home residents, veterans, and newly married couples.

I wonder if I would have been as persistent in my quest for a theological education and ultimately my ordination as a priest absent this story of moral injury. It has certainly been a driving force in my life and has pushed me through numerous obstacles to ordination in my adult life. When the Episcopal Church told me they didn't hear a call to the diaconate, I continued to search and discern what God had in mind for me. Years later, when I felt the call had reignited, I was again turned away because I wasn't ready to enroll in the seminary because of my choice to maintain my job and fund the college education of my daughter. Again, when I heard a voice telling me to pursue the path of ordained ministry, I was advised that I was too old and wouldn't be considered, that my educational credits had expired or were irrelevant and would not be accepted if I applied again to be a postulant for Holy Orders.

But, I was not to be held back. After the door was shut in my face three times, I sought ordination credentials in another denomination, the Independent Catholic Church. There I was received warmly, as though a Prodigal Son, and was ordained a deacon in August of 2015 and a priest in September of the same year. Since my ordination, I have functioned as a worker-priest, a tent maker. I regard my ministry as finding people where they are, not in churches, but in nursing homes, retirement communities, and in house churches. I convene small groups of people monthly in a House Church, a throw-back to the time of the apostles when Christians met in individuals' homes because of fear of persecution. They pray together, discuss sacred scripture, and share a meal in memory of the life of Jesus Christ of Nazareth. I help veterans tell their stories through writing workshops and minister to people with memory impairment. I look out to the margins of society and find God there among the very special people that most clergy avoid or don't even see.

My life has a thread of serving others running through it. It began in my youth and has continued in spite of attempts to thwart the achievement of my dream. Perhaps the moral injury is giving me the strength and determination to continue and find ways to bring God to others outside the tent. A story about Eldad and Medad[2] in the Hebrew Bible serves as an inspiration to me.

The author of the book of Numbers relates how God provided Moses with a special group of seventy elders who would serve as Moses's assistants in dealing with the people. The seventy were to be initiated into this role at a special rite in the tent of meeting where God would extend some of God's Spirit that was on Moses onto the elders. All proceeded according to plan as the elders were gathered with Moses in the tent. As the elders prophesied in the tent, it was reported that two men, Eldad and Medad, spoke in ecstasy in the presence of the people behind in the camp. These two elders were enrolled but did not go out into the tent. When told about the two elders prophesying outside the tent, Moses said that he wished the entire people were prophets and that God would confer his Spirit on all of them.

I am Eldad and Medad. I speak outside the tent, often maligned for being out of the mainstream, but prophesying with God's Spirit upon me.

The moral injury is important because it is central to my story. I want peace in my soul, but I don't want to forget the struggle. I want

---

2   Numbers 11:10-31 (New Revised Standard Version).

to remember that I strayed from the direction my moral compass was guiding me. I have learned from departing from my basic instincts and from the moral code that I have constructed deep in my soul.

But, this book is not just about me. I wrote it to cast a spotlight on other veterans who also were conflicted about their participation in war. I hope that it helps them name their moral injury and find ways to seek forgiveness and healing. More than anything, I hope that we can all learn to talk about war and what it does to us as individuals and as a nation.

I have offered my personal experiences to the families and friends of military veterans so that they can begin to understand the struggle that their loved ones endured in the name of service to our country. Perhaps our churches and communities will open their doors and listen to the stories of our veterans and learn from their experiences.

Acknowledgments

The writing of this memoir has been a therapeutic exercise for me that has uncovered thoughts and feelings that I never dreamed were in my subconscious mind. My purpose was to do this for me as a project toward achieving wholeness and better mental health. It was important to get it out of my gut and let me see myself in the light of day. I believe that I have accomplished my main purpose. After asking a number of people to read my manuscript, I decided to get it published and let others learn about my story. I am grateful to my beta-readers who include my brother, Gary Hattan, my lifelong friends John Glatz and Roger Skerrett, Lee Kolodziej, Luann Zanzola, Jeanine Hill-Soldner, and Bill Kruse for their encouragement to move this project forward to publication. I am indebted to Retired General James Mukoyama for his constructive criticism and attention to detail that helped me iron out the wrinkles in my story.

Thanks to Karen Skerrett who prodded me along the way to seek professional assistance in the editing and marketing of the manuscript. I am very grateful to Martha Bullen, my book adviser and coach, for helping me through the maze of selecting an editor, a book designer, and website developer. This could not have been accomplished without the discerning eye and advice of my editor, Madalyn Abrams. Madalyn helped me turn my rambling musings into a coherent, compelling story. Kudos go out to Kari Sharpe for creating an attractive website that showcases my memoir.

Very special thanks go to my spouse, Karen Blandford Hattan, for listening to my story over the past forty-four years and encouraging me to write about it. She has been a loving partner and a patient champion of all my efforts in my journey as an author, healer and minister.

Bibliography

Brock, Rita Nakashima, *Soul Repair, Recovering from Moral Injury after War.* Boston: Beacon Hill, 2012.

Hattan, Dick. "An AWOL God," Unpublished Poem, 2011.

Hattan, Dick. "178," Unpublished Poem, 2014.

Hattan, Dick. *Healing Memories.* Woodstock: Xlibris, 2010.

Hattan, Dick. "Healing Memories of War." *Journal of the Order of St. Luke* (October, 2013):8.

Hippolytus. *Apostolic Tradition*, II.16.17-19.

Khalfam, Ashfaq. "Muhammad Ali: The world's 'greatest' conscientious objector," *UTC.* June 14, 2016.13:47.

King Jr., Martin Luther. "A Time to Break Silence." In *The Essential Writings and Speeches of Martin Luther King Jr.,* edited by James M. Washington, 231-244. New York: Harper, 1986.

Leonardi, Ray. Meditation within presentation: "Healing Our Social Wounds." From the Center for Action and Contemplation. September 26, 2017.

Mahedy, William. *Out of the Night: The Spiritual Journey of Vietnam Vets.* New York: Ballantine, 1986. In Meagher, Robert Emmet, *Killing from the Inside Out.* Eugene: Cascade, 1986.

Meagher, Robert Emmet. *Killing from the Inside Out.* Eugene: Cascade, 1986.

Palmer, Parker. *Let Your Life Speak*. San Francisco: Jossey Bass, 2000.

Rohr, Richard. "Healing Our Social Wounds." From the Center for Action and Contemplation. September 26. 2017.

Tertullian. *On Idolatry,* 19.318, 321. In Meagher, Robert Emmet, *Killing from the Inside Out*. Eugene: Cascade, 1986.

About the Author

DICK HATTAN is a native of Chicago. He served in the US Army in Vietnam during 1971 with the 101st Airborne Division. He earned a Master of Management degree from Northwestern University, Kellogg School of Management in 1974 and began a forty-four year career as a health care executive. In 2013, he earned a Master of Divinity degree at Chicago Theological Seminary and was ordained a priest in the Independent Catholic Church in 2015. His ministry includes weekly liturgy at a rehabilitation and memory care center, a writer's workshop for veterans, a house church and a wedding ministry.

Hattan is married to Karen Blandford Hattan, his spouse of forty-four years. The couple has a married daughter and two grandchildren.

For more information about the author, please consult:
invisiblescarsofwar.com.